THE FAMILY OF GOD

By

Elder Lynwood Jacobs

2013

TABLE OF CONTENTS

May God bless you in the reading of these words as He did in my writing them.

Curtis Lynwood Jacobs

THE FAMILY OF GOD

"The Spirit itself beareth witness with our Spirit, that we are the children of God: And if children, then heirs; heirs of God, and joint heirs with Christ; if so be that we suffer with Him, that we may be also glorified together." (Rom. 8: 16-17) The children of God are heirs of an inheritance that is incorruptible, and undefiled, and that fadeth not away, reserved in heaven for them that are kept by the power of God through faith unto salvation ready to be revealed in the last day. (See I Peter 1: 45.) God's children are predestined unto this inheritance according to the purpose of Him who works all things after the council of His own will. (See Eph. 1:11) The heirs of promise are members of the family of God. Members of the general assembly and church of the Firstborn and the children of God are one and the same.

The apostle Paul said, "For this cause I bow my knees unto the Father of our Lord Jesus, of whom the whole family in heaven and earth is named." (Eph. 3: 14-15) This is the only place in the New Testament where the word family is mentioned. Yet, these two verses of scripture have brought me great joy when meditating about the family of God.

A natural family is made up of a father, a mother, and their offspring and is a type and shadow of the true family, the family of God. In this great and timeless family, God is the Father, Jerusalem, which is above, is the mother, and Christ and the heirs of promise are the children.

We become a member of an earthly family in one of three ways: by birth, by adoption, or by marriage. We become a member of the family of God in all three ways. A manifested child of God is born of God, adopted by God, and married to Christ.

1

"Beloved, let us love one another; for love is of God; and everyone that loveth is born of God, and knoweth God." (I John 4:7) "And will be a Father unto you, and ye shall be my sons and daughters, saith the Lord Almighty." (II Cor. 6:18) A child that is born of God is a manifested member of the family of God and has eternal life and will not come into condemnation but has passed from death unto life. We must be born again, not of a corruptible seed, but born of God, "Whosoever believeth that Jesus is the Christ is born of God, and every one that loveth Him that begat, loveth Him also that is begotten of Him." (I John 5:1) God's children love one another.

"Having predestinated us unto the adoption of children by Jesus Christ to Himself, according to the good pleasure of His will." (Eph. 1:5) God's children wait for the adoption, to wit, the redemption of their bodies. They were bought with a price; therefore, they glorify God in their body and Spirit which are God's. (See I Cor. 6:20.)

"Wherefore my brethren, ye also are become dead to the law by the body of Christ, that ye should be married to another, even Him, who is raised from the dead that we should bring forth fruit unto God." (Rom. 7:4). Those who are married to Christ and members in particular of His body, do not commit adultery by clinging to the law. Nay, they stand fast in the liberty wherewith Christ has made them free, and are no longer in bondage to the law of sin and death, but are in bondage to the law of LOVE.

Jesus said unto Mary, "Touch me not, for I am not yet ascended to my Father; but go to my brethren, and say unto them, I ascend unto my Father, and your Father, and to my God, and your God." (John 20:17) What glorious words! The risen Son of God, the one with all power in heaven and earth, sent a message by Mary that rejoices the hearts of His brethren even to this day. I am not only your Saviour, I am your Brother. God is my Father and your Father. God gave to His Son power over all flesh to give eternal life to as many as the Father gave to His Son. (See John 17:1-2.)

How wonderful it is when brethren dwell together as children of God. Their meetings are full of praise to God, and rejoicing in Christ Jesus. These children are Saints of God, and not of men. They look only to Christ as the author and finisher of their faith, and as the Shepherd and Bishop of their souls. They seek not the praise of men, but hope to manifest love according to the ordination of God's Holy will. The only order in the family of God is love and the fruits thereof.

The children of God daily take part in true communion, which is communion of the Holy Spirit. Though they are a thousand miles apart, they wash their Brethren's feet when they think of them, and see themselves as less than the least of all the Saints, if one at all. They partake of unleavened bread when they remember the nail prints in His hands, and the riven side of that broken body that perfected forever them that are sanctified. They drink of the fruit of the vine when they remember that His shed blood fulfilled a new and everlasting covenant. God's will through the Holy Spirit controls true communion, not man. Our regular communion services are a type and shadow of true communion and are a beautiful memorial service of Christ's sacrifice for the sins of His brothers and sisters, and nothing more.

God's ways are not man's ways. When we are born of our natural mother, we come forth from her and the naval cord is broken. When we are born of our spiritual mother, we enter into her and the naval cord is never broken. "But Jerusalem which is above is free, which is the Mother of us all." (Gal.

3

4:26) The apostle John, by revelation, saw his spiritual mother, New Jerusalem, coming down from God out of heaven, prepared as a bride adorned for her Husband. (See Rev. 21-22.) The apostle Paul described his spiritual mother as the general assembly and church of the first born, which are written in heaven. Mother Jerusalem and the church of the Firstborn are one with the family of God.

God's children call one another brother or sister because they believe and trust that they have the same Parents. His children love one another. Their greatest joy on earth is to be with their brethren, to be in the presence of a few of those they hope to spend eternity with at HOME. They greatly rejoice in the family reunions they are blessed to attend here on earth, and look forward with joy unspeakable to that everlasting reunion of the family of God around that great white throne in the presence of their Father God, and their beloved elder brother, Jesus Christ.

Love binds God's family together on earth as it will in that heavenly home. The doctrine of God and Christ feed God's children that are bound together by the Holy Spirit of God's love. The apostle Paul makes plain that without love, nothing else matters. "Though I speak with the tongues of men and of angels, and have not charity, I am become as sounding brass or a tinkling symbol. And though I have the gift of prophecy, and understand all mysteries and all knowledge, and though I have all faith that I could remove mountains, and have not charity, I am nothing. And though I bestow all my goods to feed the poor, and though I give my body to be burned, and have not charity, it profiteth me nothing." (I Cor. 13: 1-3)

Eloquence of speech, head knowledge of scripture, faith, offerings, and works are nothing unless each is a result of God's love ruling our thoughts and actions. If any natural urge is the source, our actions are vanity in motion, and profit nothing. Worship God and love Him, His Son, and one another are the great commandments to His children.

The Lord Almighty has promised to be a Father unto His children. What an exceeding great and precious promise! His children that He has loved with an everlasting love will be called home with their brother David to dwell in the house of the Lord forever. They will no more see through a glass darkly, but will see their Father and His Son and bask in their glorious presence throughout all eternity. "Thy dead men shall live, together with my dead body, shall they arise. Awake and sing, ye that dwell in dust, for thy dew is the dew of herbs, and the earth shall cast out the dead." (Isaiah 26:19) God's children will arise triumphant and understand, Oh death where is thy sting, oh grave where is thy victory. Our Father has given us the victory through Jesus Christ our Lord, our Friend, and our beloved Brother. They will come into their inheritance, that Kingdom prepared by God for His children.

Is the family of God ruled over by any man or groups of men? No. God's manifested will rules the thoughts and actions of His children. No man or group of men has ever had any control over the family of God. Even the apostles were subject to the will of God who works all things after the council of His own will both in heaven and in earth.

Is the family of God divided? No. They are one in Christ Jesus. Hatred, judgment, and condemnation may divide people into warring factions. Self-righteous hypocrisy may exalt one above another. Love of money or jealousy may rear their ugly heads. All are works of the flesh and do cause aggravation and heartache among the brethren who truly love one another. Satan can never stop the children of God from loving one another through every trial and temptation for their love is of God.

Is the child of God subject to man-made laws and rules of worship? No. They are not needed. God writes His laws in the mind and heart of each one of His children. These are the laws that rule the actions of a manifested child of God. A brother or sister that you love cannot offen-d you; therefore, no offense can take place between God's children.

Does the child of God know who is or who is not a brother or sister? No. Only God knows them that are His. Yet, when brethren are drawn together by love they feel that closeness and warmth that can only be felt between children of God. I believe that I have felt that closeness, which strengthens my hope that by grace I am a member of the royal family of the King.

Lynwood Jacobs

Updated 2009

FATHER

"But now, O Lord, thou art our Father, we are the clay, and thou our potter; and we all are the work of thy hand." (Isa. 64:8) Isaiah had just confessed, "But we are all as an unclean thing, and our righteousnesses are as filthy rags, and we all do fade as a leaf: and our iniquities, like the wind, have taken us away." (Isa. 64:6) Yet, in the next breath he could call God his Father, and believe that he was the work of His hands. Isaiah could only do this as he was moved by the Holy Spirit. That same Spirit tells us of our unworthiness, yet, gives us a lively hope that God is our Father, and if children, then heirs of God and joint heirs with Christ of that eternal dwelling place of the family of God.

God, our potter, can of the same lump, make one vessel unto honor and one vessel unto dishonor. Since only vessels of honor can praise, honor, and glorify Him it must be my hope to be one with them. If I was created to dishonor God, I will never receive the gift of the Holy Spirit and Christ did not pay my debt on the cross. A Father of mercy is my only hope.

"What if God, willing to show His wrath, and to make His power known, endured with much long suffering the vessels of wrath fitted to destruction: And that He might make known the riches of His glory on the vessels of Mercy which He had afore prepared unto glory, Even us, whom He hath called, not of the Jews only, but also of the Gentiles?" (Rom. 9:22-24) My hope is that He has called me, a Gentile, out of nature's darkness into the glorious liberty of the children of God, that I might praise His holy name. I believe that He has taught me that He has all power in heaven and in earth, and that Christ has power over all flesh to give eternal life to as many as the Father gave Him. Certainly it is no works on my part that gave me a hope that this lump of clay is a child of the King. If so, then my beloved Brother will come for me on that last day when He comes for His brethren to carry them home to praise Him and our Father, and His, with a perfect praise that shall never end.

Lynwood Jacobs

November 2010

CHRIST

Introduction: For whatsoever things were written aforetime were written for our learning, that we, through patience and comfort of the scriptures, might have hope. (Rom. 15:4) After Christ returned home to God, the Apostles used the references to Christ in the Old Testament to prove that He was the promised Messiah. The following are a few of these references, with the Old Testament first. The Psalms and Isaiah seem to contain more of these references than any of the others. Amazingly, they were made hundreds of years before Christ came to earth.

Psalm 139:16. Thine eyes did see my substance, yet being unperfect; and in thy book all my members were written, which in continuance were fashioned, when as yet there was none of them. (Phil.4:3, Heb.5:8, 9, Eph. 1:4) This great revelation to the Psalmist testifies that God saw the church in Christ before He was crucified to perfect His bride, and wrote their names in the Book of Life before there was an Adamic man on earth. In Phil.4:3 the Apostle Paul spoke of his fellow labourerers whose name is in the Book of Life. In Heb. 5:8, 9 the writer tells us that Christ learned obedience by the things which He suffered, and being made perfect by the things He suffered, He became the author of eternal salvation unto all them that obey Him. In Eph.1:4 Paul tells us that God chose His children in Christ before the foundation of the world.

Isa.7:14. Therefore the Lord himself shall give you a sign; Behold a virgin shall conceive, and bare a son, and shall call his name Immanuel. (Matt. 1:22, 23, Luke 1:35) In Matt. 1:22, 23 it is written, Now all this was done, that it might be fulfilled, which was spoken by the prophet, saying, Behold a virgin shall be with child, and shall bring forth a son, and they shall call his name Immanuel, which being interpreted is, God with us. In Luke 1:35 the angel of God told Mary how this would happen, that the Holy Ghost would come upon her, and the power of God would overshadow her, and that the holy thing which would be born of her would be called the Son of God.

Psalms 2:6, 7 Yet have I set my king upon my Holy hill of Zion. I will declare the decree: the Lord hath said unto me, Thou art my son; this day have I begotten thee. (Luke 1: 31- 35 and Luke 2:10, 11) God left no doubt that Christ was His Son. In Luke 1:32, 33 He told Mary that Christ would be great, and be called the Son of the Highest, and that the Lord God would give Him the throne of his father David; and that Christ would reign over the house of Jacob forever; and of His kingdom there shall be no end. In Luke 2:10,11, an angel of the Lord told the Magi to fear not, and the angel brought unto them good tidings of great joy which shall be to all the people saying, "For unto you this day is born in the city of David a Saviour which is Christ the Lord." Also, on two occasions, at His baptism, and on the Mount of Transfiguration, God spoke saying about Christ, This is my beloved son.....

Micah 5:2 But thou, Bethlehem Ephratah, though thou be little among the thousands of Judah, yet out of thee shall he come forth unto me, that is to be ruler in Israel; whose goings forth have been of old, from everlasting. The risen Christ, whose goings forth were from old, from everlasting, is the same one told of in these words in Prov. 8:22-31 (some of the most revealing words in the Bible). "The Lord possessed me in the beginning of his way, before his works of old. I was set up from everlasting, from the beginning, or ever the earth was. When there were no depths, I was brought forth, when there were no fountains abounding with water. Before the mountains were settled, before the hills was I brought forth: While as yet he had not made the earth, nor the fields, nor the highest part of the dust of the world. When he prepared the heavens, I was there, when he set a compass upon the face of the depth: When he established the clouds above: when he strengthened the fountains of the deep: When he gave to the sea his decree, that the waters should not pass his commandment: when he appointed the foundations of the earth: Then I was by him, as one brought up with him: and I was daily his delight, rejoicing always before him; Rejoicing in the habitable part of his earth; and MY DELIGHTS WERE WITH THE SONS OF MEN. In Matt.2:5, 6, Herod the king, heard the Magi were asking where is he that was born King of the Jews, and Herod demanded of the chief priests where Christ should be born. Their answer in Matt. 2:5, 6 was, "In Bethlehem of Judea: for thus it is written by the prophet, And thou Bethlehem, in the land of Juda, art not the least among the princes of Juda: for out of thee shall come a Governor, that shall rule my people Israel." Herod then plotted to find Jesus and kill Him, but it was not to be. Throughout His life Christ would say in the face of apparent danger, My time is not yet come. It was Pilate who delivered Him up to be crucified when His time came, not Herod.

There are many references in the Old Testament concerning Christ's suffering, being scorned, and death on the cross. The following are some of those with matching New Testament scriptural references.

Psalms 16:10. For thou wilt not leave my soul in hell; neither wilt though suffer thine Holy One to see corruption. (Acts 2:31 and Acts 13:35)

Psalm 22:1. My God, my God, why hast thou forsaken me? Why art thou so far from helping me, and from the words of my roaring? (Matt.27:46}

Psalm 22:6-8. But I am a worm, and no man; a reproach of men, and despised of all the people. (Rom.15:3) All they that see me laugh me to scorn: they shoot out the lip, they shake the head, saying, He trusted on the Lord that he would deliver him: let him deliver him, seeing he delighted in him. (Matt. 27:39-44, Luke 23:35,36)

Psalm 22: 16-18. For dogs have compassed me: the assembly of the wicked have enclosed me: they pierced my hands and my feet. (John 19:18, 37) I may tell all my bones: they look and stare upon me. They part my garments among them, and cast lots for my vesture. (Matt. 27:35, Luke 23:34, John 19:24).

Psalm 34:20. He keepeth all his bones: not one of them is broken. (John 19: 34, 36)

Psalm 68:18. Thou hast ascended on high, thou hast lead captivity captive: thou hast received gifts for men: for the rebellious also, that the Lord God may dwell among them. (Eph. 4:8, Acts 1:9-11) The Apostle Paul's words concerning this scripture in Eph. 4:8 tell us that when Christ ascended up on high, he led captivity captive, and gave gifts unto men. In Acts 1:9-11 are some of the most comforting words in the Bible, to me, telling of His ascension: And when He had spoken these things, while they beheld, He was taken up; and a cloud received Him out of their sight. And while they looked up steadfastly toward heaven as He went up, behold, two men stood by them in white apparel; Which also said, "Ye men of Galilee, why stand ye gazing up into heaven? This same Jesus, which is taken from you into heaven, shall come in like manner as ye have seen Him go into heaven." Glory to God! Christ Jesus is alive today in heaven, and He is coming back as He went away. Two angels of God testified to this. Christ promised to come back and get His brethren that they might be where He is now, in that land that is very far off, out beyond all worlds.

Those who have Christ in their heart, and the hope of glory, have no need for proof of His eternal existence. However, it was good when such was brought to my remembrance that Christ occupied eternity with His Father, and that I was there with Him, if I am one of those chosen in Him before the world was. Such certainly is a comfort to a convicted sinner.

Lynwood Jacobs

2011

BOOK OF LIFE

And there shall in no wise enter into it anything that defileth, neither whatsoever worketh abomination, or maketh a lie: but they which are written in the Lamb's book of life. (Rev.21:27). The "it" that only those whose names are in the Lamb's book of life shall enter, is that great city sought by Abraham, a city with foundation whose builder and maker is God. If our hope is realized we, with Abraham, will see the King in His beauty in the land that is very far off. (See Isa. 33:17.) Since it is the Lamb's book, He is the only one that can break the seals thereof.

 I believe the book mentioned in the 139th Psalm is the Lamb's book of life, "Thine eyes did see my substance, yet being unperfect, and in thy book all my members were written, which in continuance were fashioned, when as yet there were none of them." (Psalm 139:16) This tells me that every child of God had their name written in the book of life before God created Adam. Christ was the one whose substance was yet unperfect, because He had not suffered the cruel death on the cross to pay the debt that would be owed by His bride to be. (See Rev. 21:9.) Yes, He was made perfect by His suffering here on earth. "For it became Him, for whom are all things, and by whom are all things, in bringing many sons unto glory, to make the captain of their salvation perfect through suffering." (Heb. 2:10) I sure want Christ to be the Captain of the Ship of Zion that I hope will carry me across the sea of eternity. He knows the way, and has the passenger list which is in the Book of Life.

Christ appointed seventy and sent them two by two to go before Him into the cities where he was to come. The seventy returned with joy, saying, Lord even the devils are subject to us through thy name. Christ told them to rejoice not that the spirits are made subject to you, but rather rejoice that your names are written in heaven. Christ could say that because only God and He know the names in the Book of Life. (See Luke 10:17-20.) Yes, we may feel strongly that brethren who come together with us in love and peace, believing God's doctrine, and with faith in Christ Jesus, must surely have their name in the Book of Life. The Apostle Paul did the same thing, "And I entreat thee also, true yoke-fellow, help those women which laboured with me in the gospel, with Clement also, and with other my fellow-labourers, whose names are in the book of life." (Phil. 4:3) So I wouldn't be too bad if I should make a list of some of the precious brethren that I believe have their names in the Book of Life. It would bring each one to remembrance one more time.

"At that time shall Michael stand up, the great prince which standeth for the children of thy people: and there shall be a time of trouble, such as never was since there was a nation even to that same time: and at that time thy people shall be delivered, every one that shall be found written in the book." (Dan 12:1). To me this is another reference to the Lamb's Book of Life because it is speaking about God's people who shall be delivered. I believe it is also referring to Christ who shall stand for God's people in that terrible time of trouble. Daniel was blessed to tell in the next verse who many are that shall be found in the book. "And many that sleep in the dust of the earth shall awake, some to everlasting life, and some to shame and everlasting contempt." (Dan. 12:2) God's children who are asleep in Jesus will awake to everlasting life. On that last day, those who are alive and remain will be caught up with them to meet the Lord in the air and so shall they ever be with the Lord. (See I Thes. 4:13-18.)

"And whosoever was not found written in the Book of Life was cast into the lake of fire." (Rev. 21:15) Those whose names are written in the Book of Life will not be cast into the lake of fire on that last day, but will obey the voice of Him who says, "Come ye blessed of my Father, inherit the kingdom prepared for you from the foundation of the world." (Matt. 25:34) They will then go home to dwell in the house of the Lord forever with David and all of the saints of God. The last enemy, death, shall be destroyed and then the Son also himself shall be subject to Him that put all things under Him, that God may again be all in all. (See I Cor. 15: 27, 28.)

Lynwood Jacobs

2010

ELECTION

Recently, I was asked to comment on a word by word, or phrase, explanation of the book of Ephesians. Since it was obvious early on that the King James Version was not being used, it gave me an excuse to read only a small measure of the writing. However, the author's failure to comment on a part of Eph.1:4 intrigued me. He wrote, "He chose us--We come now to another mystery. There has been so much debate and discord among believers over the issue of election." That was the author's only comment on "He chose us," or "election."

The doctrine of election is not a mystery to the true believers to whom it has been revealed by the Holy Spirit. God chose us in His son before the foundation of the world, if we are one of His children. From the beginning, God ordained the saving grace in Christ Jesus for each one His children, that they would be holy and without blame before Him in love throughout eternity. He hath made each one of us for the purpose that He has in us. We did not make ourselves. At God's appointed time His children receive the gift of the Holy Ghost. (Rom. 5:5) It is this Spirit that is the love of God in their hearts and minds that changes their walk, their talk, and their thoughts. It is this Spirit that gives them wisdom and revelation in the knowledge of God and Jesus Christ. It is this Spirit that makes them manifested, born-again children of the King. Saul of Tarsus' experience on the road to Damascus, and his conversion to become Paul, the Apostle to the Gentiles, is an excellent example of how the manifestation of God's love and power can change one's life.

Christ spoke of the elect. When He described the horrors of the abomination of desolation, spoken of by Daniel the prophet, He closed with these words, "And except those days should be shortened, there should no flesh be saved: but for the elect's sake those days shall be shortened." (Matt. 24:15-24) In a stronger assertion of the same theme, Christ said, "And except that the Lord had shortened those days, no flesh should be saved: but for the elect's sake, whom HE HATH CHOSEN, He hath shortened the day's." (Mark 13:14-20) The chosen elect of God and Christ are not forsaken in this world, neither in the world to come.

Christ warned, "For false Christs and false prophets shall rise, And shall shew signs and wonders, to seduce, if it were possible, even the elect." (Mark 13:22) Only the blood of Christ, and the manifesting of the Holy Spirit can save a soul from death. Those claiming to save souls are the false prophets spoken of here. For anyone to deny the power of the God-given Holy Spirit in saving souls is blasphemy, and will not be forgiven neither in this world, neither in the world to come. (This includes James 5:19, 20) It is impossible for those who were once enlightened, and have tasted of the heavenly gift, and were made partakers of the Holy Ghost, and have tasted of the good word of God, and the power of the world to come, if they should fall away to renew them unto repentance, seeing they crucify the Son of God afresh and put him to an open shame.

The Apostle Peter believed in the election of God. In his letter to the elect according to the foreknowledge of God the Father, through sanctification of the Spirit, he called them a chosen generation, a royal priesthood, an holy nation, a peculiar people, that they should show forth the praises of Him who called them out of nature's darkness into His marvelous light. (See Peter 1:2 and Peter 2:9.) When His light shines in their soul, God's elect praise, honor, and glorify Him and His precious son, Jesus Christ. They bless them because theirs is the power, and riches, and wisdom, and strength, and honor, and blessing. (See Rev. 5:12.) Except the electing grace of Almighty God and the saving grace in Christ Jesus is ours, we are of the unbelieving non-elect. My hope is that I have ever been one with my brethren in Christ Jesus, who also was chosen of God, and precious. (1 Peter 2:4)

The Apostle Paul believed in the election wherein God chose His children. In a letter unto the church of the Thessalonians in God our Father and the Lord Jesus Christ he wrote, "But we are bound to give thanks always to God for you, brethren beloved of the Lord, because God hath from the beginning chosen you to salvation through sanctification of the Spirit and belief of the truth:" (2 Thes. 2:13) First, let me emphasize, these words apply to the church today as they did in the Apostle Paul's day. God hath from the beginning chosen the beloved members of His church to be sanctified (set apart) by the gift of His Spirit and belief in Christ, in every age of time from Adam until the last day. Every member of the general assembly and church of the firstborn, which are written in heaven, are sure to go home on the last day to dwell in the house of the Lord forever.

The Apostle Paul asked, "Who shall lay anything to the charge of God's elect? It is God that justifieth." How does God justify the elect? "Being justified freely by His grace through the redemption that is in Christ Jesus." (Rom. 4:25.) "Therefore being justified by faith, we find peace with God through our Lord Jesus Christ: By whom also we have access by faith into this grace wherein we stand and rejoice in hope of the glory of God." (Rom. 5:1) For we are saved by hope, but hope that is seen is not hope....(Rom.

8:24) Faith is a gift of God to His elect. Christ is their hope, their saviour. He is their Lord, their righteousness, yea, their all in all.

In Paul's letter to all that be in Rome, beloved of God, called to be saints, the Apostle spoke of the election many times. He spoke of "the purpose of God according to election." (Rom.9:11) He spoke of the election of Grace, (Rom. 11:5), and that touching the election they are beloved. (Rom.11:28) The scriptures have other references to the election and choices of God, an eternal fact.

(All scriptures referred to here are from the King James Version of the Bible which is 400 years old this year having first appeared in 1611. My ancestor, Nicholas Jacob, and his family came from England to the Plymouth, Massachusetts area in 1633. He probably did not have a copy of the KJV, but he could have.)

Lynwood Jacobs

May 2011

COMFORTER

Christ speaks of the Comforter in four verses of scripture recorded by the Apostle John. These words of truth are believed by the ones who have received the Comforter.

"But the Comforter, which is the Holy Ghost, whom the Father will send in my name, he shall teach you all things, and bring all things to your remembrance, whatsoever I have said unto you." (John 14:26) The Comforter is the Holy Ghost, a gift of God to His elect only, to teach them all things that God has chosen to reveal of Himself and His Son. Paul described the Comforter as a Spirit of wisdom and revelation in the knowledge Him, the eyes of their understanding being enlightened, that they might know what is the hope of His calling, and what is the riches of His glory in the Saints. (See Eph.1:17, 18.) The Holy Ghost is not a spirit of the world, but the Spirit which is of God by which His children know the things that are freely given them of God.

"And I will pray the Father, and He shall give you another Comforter, that he may abide with you forever; even the Spirit of Truth: whom the world cannot receive, because it seeth Him not, neither knoweth Him, but ye know Him, for he dwelleth with you, and shall be in you." (John 14:16, 17) Once received, the Comforter which is the Spirit of Truth will abide with you forever. There is no backsliding, because the Holy Ghost brings to you the love of God, the most powerful force in this world. When God's love exercises His children, they bring forth fruit unto God and the end everlasting life. The fruit of the flesh cannot substitute for the fruit of the Spirit.

"Nevertheless I tell you the truth; It is expedient for you that I go away: for if I go not away the Comforter will not come unto you: but if I depart, I will send him unto you." (John 16:7)

Christ comforted His disciples while He was with them, but now He must depart for a little while, else the Comforter would not come. He died and rose from the dead and returned to where He was before. Before He departed, He breathed on His disciples and they received the Holy Ghost. (John 20:22) This presents a great puzzle. Between the time that He told Mary not to touch Him because He had not yet ascended unto the Father, and then later told His disciples to touch Me and see for a Spirit hath not flesh and bone as you see Me have, did He go to and return from His Father? All things are possible with God!

"But when the Comforter is come, whom I will send unto you from the Father, even the Spirit of Truth, which proceedeth forth from the Father, and he shall testify of me. Christ testified that the Holy Ghost proceeds from the Father unto His brethren. He said that the Holy Ghost testifies of Him. The natural man receiveth not the things of the Holy Ghost for they are foolishness unto him; neither can he know them for they are Spiritually discerned. To say that the devil wants me and God wants me, so it is up to me to choose one or the other is pure hogwash. God chose me in His son before the world began, or He didn't. I want know whether my name is in the Book of Life until it is called on the last day. If the Spirit of Truth is the source of my belief it needs no defense, but if not, it can't be defended. My hope is that I have been blessed of God to speak and believe the Truth, that I have been given to love, praise, honor and glorify Him and His beloved son, Jesus Christ.

Lynwood Jacobs

February 2011

ELECT

The Apostle Peter spoke of the "elect according to the foreknowledge of God the Father." (See I Peter 1:2.) The Apostle Paul said that whom God did foreknow, (the elect) He also did predestinate to be conformed to the image of His Son, that He might be the firstborn among many brethren. (See Rom. 8:29.) Christ's brethren are the elect that God predestinated to be conformed to the image of His Son. The elect were chosen in Christ by God before the foundation of the world. (See Eph. 1:4&5.) God made the choice of the elect according to the good pleasure of His will. All this tells me that the election was held in the ancients of eternity and that it was God the Father who chose and ordained unto eternal life every one of His children, when as yet there was none of them. Does the child choose eternal life? No! God, who cannot lie, promised eternal life in Christ to His elect before the world began.

The Apostle Paul asked, "Who shall lay anything to the charge of God's elect?" He answered his question by adding, it is God that justifieth. How are the elect justified in this sin cursed world? "Being justified freely by His grace through the redemption that is in Christ Jesus." (Rom. 4:24) Therefore being justified by faith we find peace with God through Jesus Christ. Faith in God and Christ through grace is a gift of God that justifies the elect only. The elect are born again, born of God, born of the Holy Spirit and come forth as manifest children of the King.

Christ warned, "For false Christs and false prophets shall rise. And shall shew signs and wonders, to seduce, if it were possible, even the elect." (Mark. 13:22) Only Christ's blood and the Holy Spirit can save a soul from death. Those claiming to be able to do this are the false Christs spoken of here. To deny the power of the Holy Spirit in the new birth is blasphemy, and will not be forgiven neither in this world, neither in the world to come. God's elect are the sheep that are known to Christ and hear His voice and follow Him and no other.

Christ said, "And then shall they see the Son of man coming in the clouds with great power and glory, And then shall He send His angels, and shall gather together His elect from the four winds, from the uttermost part of the earth to the uttermost part of heaven. (Mark 13:26, 27) When all of the elect have been gathered together they will see Christ fulfill, "Come ye blessed of our Father, inherit the Kingdom prepared for you." Then cometh the end when Christ shall deliver up the Kingdom to the Father. Christ will then lay down all rule and all authority and power that God the Father may again be all in all. (See I Cor. 15:26-28 and John 14:1-3.) Death is conquered and every Saint is perfected and delivered up to praise and glorify the Father and the Son in that bright land that shall never end. I hope to be there with you.

Lynwood Jacobs

August 2009

TEMPLE OF GOD

Know ye not that ye are the temple of God, and that the Spirit of God dwelleth in you? (I Cor.3:16) The Apostle Paul rebuked the churches at Corinth more than any others he had established. It seems that the leaders of these churches were prone to go astray, even denying the resurrection. Here it seems that they are denying Christ's purifying blood that bought them with a price on a cross on Calvary's hill. Maybe a little free-willism, or denying the power of the Holy Ghost had crept in. Like they say, there is nothing new under the sun. Later Paul spoke firmly, "What? Know ye not that your body is a temple of the Holy Ghost, which is in you, which ye have of God, and ye are not your own? For ye are bought with a price; therefore glorify God in your body and in your Spirit, which are God's. (I Cor. 6:19, 20) Our natural body is given to us of God, to serve His purpose in us on earth. Our natural body becomes a temple of God on earth only if Christ bought it with a price, His death on the cross, and the Spirit of God has entered therein. Christ did not die on the cross to save Spirits. Children of God may not all sleep, but all will be changed. In the resurrection on the last day their bodies will be raised spiritual bodies, fashioned like unto the glorious body of Christ, that it may be reunited with their Holy Spirit as a Temple of God forevermore.

On Mars hill the Apostle Paul preached an unknown God to the men of Athens, "God that made the world and all things therein, seeing that He is Lord of heaven and earth, dwelleth not in temples made with hands; neither is worshipped with men's hands, as though He needed anything, seeing He giveth to all, life, and breath, and all things." (See Acts 17: 22-25.) It seems from this that these great temples of vanity we see that are made with men's hands are not occupied by God, and all their collections to help God are for naught. I hope that we are thankful for our family meeting houses and the comfort they afford in all kinds of weather, but Sunday is only one of the seven days in a week when His children worship God. May He also bless us to know that it is we that need Him, and that He has never been the little begging, wanting, will-if- you- let-him god of delusion so abroad in the land.

In another letter to the Corinthians, Paul expresses why I hope that I am now a temple of the living God, "And what agreement hath the temple of God with idols? For ye are the temple of the living God; as God hath said, I will dwell in them, and walk in them, and I will be their God, and they shall be my people." (II Cor. 6:16) Hopefully, I will never again agree with idols. I have no confidence in the flesh, and fully trust none but God and Christ. I have a hope that I am a manifested child of God and feel that I have been blessed to walk with my brethren in peace, love, and fellowship on this earth. Great is God's mercy, and His ways past finding out! That is why my hope is so precious to me.

Lynwood Jacobs

2010

EPHESIANS 3:16-21

To me, one of the most profound passages of scripture in the Bible is Ephesians 3:16-21. The hope that such could apply to an unworthy one as I am brings great joy. I believe it is the Apostle Paul's prayer for his brethren whom he loved.

Paul prayed, "that He would grant you, according to the riches of His glory, to be strengthened with might by His spirit in the inner man; that Christ may dwell in your hearts by faith; that ye, being rooted and grounded in love, may be able to comprehend with all the saints what is the breadth, and length, and depth, and height; and to know the love of Christ, which passeth knowledge, that ye might be filled with all the fullness of God. Now unto Him that is able to do exceeding abundantly above all that we ask or think, according to the power that worketh in us, Unto Him be glory in the church by Christ Jesus throughout all ages, world without end."

Oh, the depth of the riches both of the wisdom and knowledge of God, how unsearchable are His judgments and His ways past finding out. How glorious are the riches of God's grace by which saints are saved by the workings of His mighty power. (A manifested child of God is a saint of God.) It gives their sin-weary souls a hope in the redeeming blood of Christ that takes away sin and leaves the manifested children of God as white as snow. When the love of God is shed abroad in sinners hearts by the Holy Ghost which is given them of God, it turns their world upside down and they love things they once hated, and hate things they once loved. It gives them hope of eternal life in Christ and faith in His Father and theirs, and gives them a desire for that life and immortality that Christ brought to light through the gospel of peace.

The Holy Spirit is not a spirit of the world, but the Spirit which is of God. It is by this Spirit that saints know the things that are freely given them of God, which things also they speak, not in words which man's wisdom teacheth but which the Holy Ghost teacheth, comparing Spiritual things with Spiritual. Saints glory in their heavenly Father and His Son Jesus Christ and none other. They rejoice in the love of God in their heart that will bind them to their brethren, to Christ, and to God forever, world without end.

Lynwood Jacobs

February 2010

SOUL

The soul is the spiritual makeup of a human being. In every human there is the spirit of man and an evil spirit. If they are born again of God, they also possess the Holy Spirit. These three spirits make up the soul of a manifested child of God here on earth.

We know the things of man by the spirit of man which is in every human to the degree ordained of God. This is the Spirit that God gave to Adam, and Adam became a living soul, a living, breathing human being. It separates all mankind from every other living creature. The better fruits of this spirit might be a parent's natural love for their child, a child's respect for its parents, respect for the property rights of others, and a helpful hand to a neighbor.

We are tempted by the same evil spirit that tempted in the beginning. It is called a serpent, Satan, a devil, and other names for the same evil spirit created by God to lie and tempt. The fruits of this spirit might be a parents abuse of their child, children who have no respect for their parents, theft of that which is not yours, or refusal to help a neighbor in need.

God's elect receive the gift of the Holy Spirit when they are born again of God. The fruits of this Spirit might be parents who worship God and love their children as though they were children of God, children who worship God and love their parents as though they were children of God, a real respect for all the rights of others, and a thankful, loving heart for your neighbors.

When the body of a non-elect dies the soul dies with it. The natural part of the soul is temporal.

When the body of a child of God goes to sleep, the Holy Spirit is their living soul that returns to God who gave it to await the morning of the resurrection when it will be reunited with their spiritual body. They will then come forth in the image and after the likeness of their beloved elder brother, Jesus Christ. The Spiritual part of the soul is eternal.

Lynwood Jacobs

2009

DOCTRINE

Doctrine as defined here comprises those religious principles that we are taught to believe. There are four distinct doctrines mentioned in the Bible. All others may be placed under one or the other of these four:

1. The doctrine of God. John 7:16

2. The principles of the doctrine of Christ. Heb. 6:1

3. The doctrine of men. Matt. 15:9

4. The doctrine of devils. I Tit. 4:1

Jesus said, "My doctrine is not mine, but His that sent me." That doctrine which tells of God's omnipotent power, electing grace, eternal glory, perfect work, and manifested will, love, and mercy is God's doctrine. God's doctrine exalts God and abases man. His doctrine is truth and is taught by God to the children of God.

In Hebrews it is written, "Therefore leaving the principles of the doctrine of Christ...." That doctrine which ascribes to Christ His God-given power and glory, saving grace, finished work, and manifested love is Christ's doctrine. His doctrine exalts Christ and abases man. Christ's doctrine is Truth and is taught by Christ to His brethren, the children of God.

Jesus said, "Howbeit in vain do they worship Me, teaching for doctrines the commandments of men." Man's doctrine attempts to exalt man and abase God. Man's doctrine is a lie and is taught by man to the children of men.

Paul wrote to Timothy, "Now the Spirit speaketh expressly, that in the latter times some shall depart from the faith, giving heed to seducing spirits, and doctrines of devils." That doctrine which attempts to exalt man and God equally

devil's doctrine and is much
ie. A seducing spirit teaches
ded. His doctrine is such a
ie that it would fool the very

t" doctrine because he often
attaches a lie to the truth.
re as follows:

ut it is up to you to believe.
ut the truth is we believe
ig of God's mighty power.
said this is the work of God
i whom He has sent. (See

nings, but he predestinated
iod did foreknow all things,
ed all things that occur in
following are some "bad"
d as being from God:

er to destroy. (Isa. 54:16)

Ie formed the crooked
3)

i things of the world. (I Cor.

nings of the world. (I Cor.

e. God chose the things that are despised. (I Cor. 1:27)

f. God created evil. (Isa. 45:7)

g. God sent a lying spirit into the mouth of Ahab's prophets. (I Kings 22:22)

h. God created darkness. (Isa. 45:7)

i. To everything there is a season, and a time to every purpose under heaven. (See Ecc. 3:1. Ecc. 3:2-8.)

j. In this life you will have tribulation. (See John 16:33.)

3. Faith is a gift of God, but it is up to us to exercise that faith. Faith is a gift of God, and when worked by the Holy Spirit, true faith gives substance to the things hoped for and becomes the evidence of things not seen. Faith exercises God's children.

4. Christ is head over all things to the church, but it is up to man to keep the church clean and in order. Christ is head over all things to the church and His love rules our actions to give order in the church. The love of God is the most powerful force in the universe and it unites brethren with an unbreakable bond that knows no bounds.

5. Salvation is alone of the Lord, but it is up to you to accept Christ as your personal saviour. Salvation is alone of the Lord, and if God made you accepted in

the Beloved He was your personal Saviour before the world began. The result is that you will be born again of God in this life. This new birth gives you a Spirit of wisdom and knowledge of God. Therefore, you cannot blaspheme the Holy Ghost by denying the power thereof.

There is no need for the devil's doctrine to be taught to worldly congregations, so he attempts to spread his doctrine among God's people. That is why Saints try the spirits. Do they ascribe greatness unto God and Christ, or do they attempt to exalt man or some mixture of man's work and God's grace? It is all of grace.

Man's doctrine is simple. It declares a wanting little god that begs, wants, wishes, and will-if-you let him, but has little or no power. Such a little god might want me to do something and if I refused, he could do nothing about it. Vanity could then exalt me above such a puny god. That is the purpose of man's doctrine. It so blatantly attempts to exalt man above God that even the youngest of God's manifested children will soon see through such lies.

The crowning principle of the doctrine of Christ tells us that God gave to His beloved son power over all flesh to give eternal life to as many as God gave to His son. (See John 17:1.) This is from the words of Christ who is the very Word of God, and we are exhorted by God to hear Him. God crowned His Son with honor and glory and exalted His name above every name but His own. The principles of the doctrine of Christ declare the freedom of the church from dead works to serve the living God in spirit and in truth. Christ has saved His people and at the appointed time He calls each one of them with a Holy calling, not according to their works but according to His own purpose and grace which was given to them in Him before the world began. Christ's doctrine teaches His loved ones that they are to look to Him as the author and finisher of their faith and as the true Shepherd and Bishop of their soul, and to no other.

Oh! How wondrous is the doctrine of God! The psalmist cried out, "All Thy works shall praise thee, O Lord; and thy Saints shall bless Thee. They shall speak of the glory of Thy Kingdom and talk of Thy power. Thy Kingdom is an everlasting Kingdom, and Thy dominion endureth throughout all generations. The Lord is righteous in ALL His ways and is holy in ALL His work. God has made known unto His people His mighty acts and the glorious majesty of His Kingdom which is timeless, eternal, unchanging and which shall stand forever.

God's doctrine perfectly abases man. When confronted with the majesty of His ways, Job felt only an awesome silence flood his soul. Man's condition must be revealed to him by God because the natural man cannot stand to be abased. Man will exalt himself as high as the eagle and make his nest among the stars. He will reject and fight any doctrine that condemns his self-righteous hypocrisy which comes from a holier than thou attitude. Even a child of God whom God has brought forth out of the dregs of humanity will become a self-appointed judge and jury over his peers if not kept from doing so by the manifested will and power of God. A holier-than-thou attitude can afflict sorely at any time, and when this evil appears among God's people, it can be matched only by jealousy and money in causing distress among the brethren.

We can fault no one for the doctrine they have been taught to believe. If taught of the Spirit, we will believe true doctrine. If not, what difference does it make whether we believe the lies of the Nicolaitenes or of the Pharisees, or the doctrine of men or devil's?

The doctrine of predestination ascribes greatness unto our God with unmatched power, clarity and beauty. All other principles of the doctrine of God our Saviour are founded upon the foreknowledge and manifestation of the determinate council of God. Not only is our eternal destination, which we hope to be that Kingdom on high prepared by God already determined, but our destiny in this life is already determined by God who works all things after the council of His own will.

May God reveal His precious doctrine in our heart. Hopefully, He has blessed us to reject all other doctrines. The purpose of the church is to render unto God that glory that He will not give to another, and to praise Him, honor Him, and glorify Him even in this present world. In the world to come, may we praise Him in His glorious presence forevermore.

Lynwood Jacobs

Undated

GIFTS OF GOD

The gift of eternal life:

My sheep hear my voice, and I know them, and they follow me: and I give unto them eternal life: and they shall never perish, neither shall any man pluck them out of my hand. (John 10:27, 28) Christ has always known His sheep, even when God chose them in Him before the foundation of the world. Here He speaks of His brethren as sheep, and Himself as the good Shepherd calling them out and leading them to green pasture. Here he tells his brethren of the Father's great gift to them, the gift of eternal life secured by His promise that they shall never perish. And this is the record that God has given us eternal life, and this life is in His Son. (1 John 5:11) This is my hope, that this wonderful gift of eternal life has been given to one who knows his unworthiness.

God's gift of His Son:

For God so loved the world that He gave His only begotten Son, that whosoever believeth in Him should not perish but have everlasting life. John 3:16. This promise of the greatest gift of all is to those who believe as the Apostle Paul says in Eph.1:19 "And what is the exceeding greatness of His power to us-ward who believe according to the working of His mighty power." In Acts 13:48 we are told that "… as many as were ordained unto eternal life believed." It is plain that everlasting life through Christ is for the children of God only, the believers who were chosen of God in the ancients of eternity to be made manifest in this time world. These are they who believe in Christ and His sacrifice, death on the cross, that His brethren might have life and have it more abundantly.

These are they that are born of God and believe in their heart that Jesus is the Christ, the Son of God.

God's gift of the Holy Ghost:

And hope maketh not ashamed; because the love of God is shed abroad in our hearts by the Holy Ghost which is given unto us. (Rom. 5:5) The gift of this immortal Spirit to a child of God is the new birth that makes the receiver a manifest child of the King. Such a one can never be ashamed of the electing grace of God, and the saving grace of Jesus Christ. The Saints of old could not deny their Savior, even when faced with death in the lion's den or tied to the burning stake or being stoned to death. They certainly knew the trials and tribulations that Christ said that we would have in his world. (See Heb.11:35-40.)

God's gift of the Kingdom:

Fear not, little flock; for it is your Father's good pleasure to give you the kingdom. (Luke 12:32) The King rules in righteousness over His kingdom which was His to give to His little flock. Christ said my Kingdom is not of this world. (John 18:36) His brethren are not of the world even as he is not of the world. (John 17:16) Then cometh the end, when He shall have delivered up the Kingdom to God, even the Father…(I Cor. 15:24) Every embodied Saint will have finally reached HOME, their journey is over. Now the dark glass is removed and they know as they are known, and see as they are seen.

God's gift of Preaching

Whereof I was made a minister, according to the gift of the grace of God given unto me by the effectual working of His power. Unto me, who am less than the least of all the Saints, is this grace given, that I should preach among the Gentiles the unsearchable riches of Christ; (Eph. 3:7,8)

Just as all things, preaching is a gift of God. The preaching of the unsearchable riches of Christ is too precious and needful to God's children to be left to the imagination of men. God-called ministers preach the Truth that praises, honors and glorifies the triune Godhead. A wishing, wanting, will-if-you-let-him little god proffered by man-made ministers is an abomination to God and His children. For there are certain men crept in unawares, who were before of old ordained to this condemnation, ungodly men, turning the grace of our God into lasciviousness, and denying the only God, and our Lord Jesus Christ. Jude:4. We can only hope that we are not one of those ordained of old to be wanton, lewd, lustful and ungodly in the name of religion The Apostle Paul prayed for that Spirit of wisdom and revelation in the knowledge of God that we might know the riches of His grace in His kindness toward us through Jesus Christ. Without that Spirit of love and wisdom in us, no matter how eloquent the words, they are as sounding brass and a tinkling symbol.

God's gift of faith

For by grace are ye saved through faith; and that not of yourselves: it is the gift of God. (Eph.2: 8) Faith is for those who have a lively hope in a living God and His son, Jesus Christ. Faith is the substance of things hoped for, the evidence of things not seen. True faith which worketh by love gives substance to our hope in the gifts and promises of God.

Christ's gift of peace.

And the peace of God, which passeth all understanding, shall keep your hearts and minds through Christ Jesus. (Phil. 4:7) Peace I leave with you, my peace I give unto you: not as the world giveth, give I unto you. Let not your heart be troubled, neither let it be afraid. (John 14:27) When God reconciles us to His will then we know that peace that passeth all understanding.

For the gifts and calling of God are without repentance. (Rom. 11:29) His gifts and calling were ordained of God before the world began. Repentance from sin and dead works to serve the living God comes during one's calling, not before. God's children are called out of nature's darkness into the glorious liberty of the children of God. They are called with a Holy calling, not according to their works but according to God's purpose and grace given to them in Christ before the world began. They that are in the flesh cannot worship God in Spirit and in Truth. But we are not in the flesh but in the Spirit if so be the Spirit of God dwell in us. Then, and only then can we worship God in Spirit and in Truth, and rejoice in the joy of His gifts and calling.

What do we have that we have not received of God? Nothing! Every hour of darkness, every moment of rapture, every time of heart ache and sadness, every time of joy and sweet communion with our brethren, every ache and pain both physical and emotional, every natural and every spiritual blessing, all come down from our heavenly Father to prepare His family for their eternal HOME.

Lynwood Jacobs

October 2008

GRAVES

"Therefore prophesy and say unto them, Thus saith the Lord God; Behold, O my people, I will open your graves, and cause you to come up out of your graves, and bring you into the land of Israel. And ye shall know that I am the Lord, when I have opened your graves, O my people, and brought you up out of your graves, And shall put my Spirit in you, and ye shall live, and I shall place you in your own land: then shall you know that I the Lord have spoken it, and performed it, saith the Lord." (Eze. 37:12-14) Ezekiel spoke as he was led by the Spirit of God to make what to me is a clear prophesy about the resurrection on the last day. Prophesy came not in old time by the will of man, but Holy men of old spake as they were moved by the Holy Ghost. (See 2 Peter 1:21.) Since it was the Spirit of God that caused Ezekiel to prophesy, I believe he was prophesying of Spiritual things.

God promised to bring His people up out of the grave and place them in their own land. What land is their own land? I believe it is that land that Isaiah was prophesying about when he was inspired by the Holy Ghost to say, "Thine eye shall see the King in his beauty, they shall behold the land that is very far off." (Isaiah was blessed to speak about this very same thing.) Thy dead men shall live, together with my dead body shall they arise, ... and the earth shall cast out the dead.." (Isa.26:19). It is a land where they will eat freely of the fruit of the Tree of Life and live forever. Nothing about that land is temporal, but all is eternal. Faith and hope will be gone for the new inhabitants will now see as they are seen, and know as they are known. There is a River in that land; the streams thereof make glad the city of God. This is the River of Life and those who drink from its streams live forever.

It is plain that this is written for a special people, the people of God. It was not written to the world. Who are God's people? They are those that are asleep in Christ in the grave. They are members of the family of God. They are members of the general assembly and Church of the first born, which have their names in the Book of Life. They are Christ's brethren, those that He died for. They are those that God chose in Christ Jesus before the world began. They are those that love one another, love God, and love His Son. They are those whose sins were imputed to Christ in a covenant with His Father, and that have ever been holy and without blame before God in love. They are those that have been born again, born of the Spirit, and received eternal life as a gift of God.

Lynwood Jacobs

2011

That body that was sown in the grave was a natural body. When God brings it up out of the grave, it will be raised a spiritual body. It was sown in corruption; it will be raised in incorruption. It was sown in weakness; it will be raised in power. It was sown in dishonor, it will be raised a glorified body. God will put His Spirit in that incorruptible, glorified body that will come forth in the image of His Son at the command of Christ on the last day. This Spirit is the one that returned unto God from that natural temple of the Holy Ghost that was put in the grave. That body raised by God will forever be a living temple of the Holy Ghost. This embodied Spiritual being with all the children of God will go home to forever render perfect praise, honor, and glory unto their Father.

Lynwood Jacobs

July 2011

ETERNAL LIFE

"My sheep hear my voice, and I know them, and they follow me: And I give unto them eternal life; and they shall never perish, neither shall any man pluck them out of my hand." (John 10:27, 28). Eternal life is a gift ordained by God, made possible by Christ, and made manifest by the Holy Ghost. Receivers of this gift are Christ's sheep, known unto Him from everlasting. In a Psalm of praise, the writer was inspired to write "Know ye not that the Lord He is God: it is He that made us and not we ourselves: we are His people, and the sheep of His pasture." (Psalm 100: 3) In a vision, the prophet Daniel saw one like the Son of man come to the Ancient of days, And there was given Him dominion, and glory, and a kingdom, that all people, nations, and languages, should serve Him: His dominion is an everlasting dominion, which shall not pass away, and His kingdom that which shall not be destroyed." (See Daniel 7: 13, 14.) Christ verified Daniel when speaking unto His God, "Father, the hour is come; glorify thy Son, that thy Son may also glorify thee: As thou hast given Him power over all flesh, that He should give eternal life to as many as thou hast given Him." (See John 17:1, 2.)

The Apostle Paul wrote this to Titus, one that he called mine own son after the common faith, "In hope of eternal life, which God, that cannot lie, promised before the world began." (See Titus 1:2, 4.) Eternal, everlasting, timeless, endless life was promised to the elect Saints of God, before God formed this special little world out on the edge of His vast universe. Why? How unsearchable are His judgments and His ways past finding out! Maybe it just seemed good in His sight and He gets pleasure out of it. We hope that we are one of the children of promise that the Apostle Peter described thusly, "For the promise is unto you, and to your children, and to all that are afar off, even as many as the Lord our God shall call." (Acts 2:39) We hope that God has called us out of nature's darkness into the glorious liberty of the children of God. Praise God that when on earth, Christ would say concerning His sheep, "And other sheep I have which are not of this fold: them also I must bring, and they SHALL hear my voice; and there SHALL be one fold, and one Shepherd." (John 10:16) My hope is that God ordained me to be a member of Christ's sheepfold.

Christ told the Samaritan woman at Jacob's well, "Whosoever drinketh of this water shall thirst again: But whosoever drinketh of the water that I shall give him shall never thirst; but the water that I shall give him shall be in him a well of water springing up into everlasting life." (See John 4:13, 14.) What a wonderful gift is living water to one who has been made, by the Holy Spirit, to thirst after righteousness. When filled with living water they taste of that righteousness, joy, and peace that He alone can give. They are made reconciled that "Thy will be done in earth as it is in heaven," one of the things we are told to pray for in what is called by some, the Lord's prayer. (See Mathew 6:9-13.) To beg "not Thy will but my will be done in earth" is the fruit of darkness.

Paul sent this to all that be in Rome, beloved of God, called to be Saints, "But now being made free from sin, and become servants to God, ye have your fruit unto holiness, and the end everlasting life. For the wages of sin is death, but the gift of God is eternal life through Jesus Christ our Lord." When God calls one to Sainthood by Christ Jesus, that one will answer the call. God calls with irresistible power, yea, a holy calling, not according to our works, but according to His own purpose and grace which was given us in Christ Jesus before the world began. I cannot account myself worthy of such grace except Christ is my righteousness. If we say that we have no sin, we deceive ourselves, and the truth is not in us. If we say we have not sinned, we make Him a liar, and His word is not in us. (See I John 1:8, 10.) God made Christ, who knew no sin, to be sin for us, that we might be made the righteousness of God in Him. (See II Cor. 5:25.) His own righteousness is the only kind acceptable unto God. That is why we hope that Christ is the "Lord our righteousness." (See I Cor. 1:30.)

Christ stressed the point that He came down from heaven to do the will of the Father. (See John 6:36.) In two verses He tells us what the Father's will is toward His family. In the first He said that all of which He has given Me I should lose nothing, but should raise it up again at the last day. In the next verse, Christ makes it plain that everyone that seeth the Son and believeth on Him may have everlasting life, and He will raise them up on the last day. (See John 6:39, 40.) On that last day God's faithful children, though asleep, will come forth with an incorruptible, glorified, spiritual body with power to ascend on high, a body that will be an everlasting temple of their Holy Spirit given them of God. Then, and only then, can we say with a surety "Surely goodness and mercy has followed me all the days of my life, and I will now dwell in the house of the Lord forever."

Oh, the depth of the riches, both of the wisdom and knowledge of God, how unsearchable are His judgments, and His ways past finding out. This is the God who made this world and all things therein, seeing He is Lord of heaven and of earth. He is not worshipped in Temples made with hands, neither is He worshipped with men's hands as though He needed anything. It is He that hath determined before the times appointed! Know ye not that your body is a temple of the Holy Ghost which is of God, and ye are not your own, for ye are bought with a price; therefore glorify God in your body and Spirit, which are God's. Is this too great a load to bear? Never fear, there is one whose yoke is easy and His burden is light for those that love God and truly believe that Jesus Christ is the Son of God. Beloved, love one another. God has loved you with an everlasting love if you are one of His children. He has never left you, or forsaken you. It is He who has given you eternal life in His Son.

Lynwood Jacobs

2009

SLEEP

I would not have you to be ignorant brethren concerning
them that are asleep, even as others who have no hope.
(See I Thes. 4:13-18.) One that is asleep will wake up!
Lazarus was asleep. He woke up, and arose at the
command of his Savior and the grave clothes were removed
from him. (John 11:43, 44) Lazarus' sickness was unto
natural death, for the glory of God, that the Son of God
might be glorified thereby. Men thought Lazarus was
eternally perished because there is a sickness unto death.
Martha, his sister, grieved until Christ proved, "Thy brother
shall rise again."

I believe that every one of God's children who are asleep in
Jesus will rise again. Who are they? He that believeth in
Me, though he were dead yet shall he live. As many as
were ordained unto eternal life believe. Whosoever liveth
and believeth in Me shall never die. Sleep, yes, though a
1000 years on the highest mountain, yet they will rise at
His command. He gives unto believer's eternal life and
they shall never perish. The story of Lazarus shows Christ's
power over all flesh to give eternal life to as many as God
gave to Him. He has the same power now that He had then.
(See John 17:1, 2.)

Lazarus had both a natural existence and a Spiritual
existence. When Christ said Lazarus is dead, it meant his
natural existence had ended. That will happen to all of us.
When Christ said that Lazarus sleepeth, it meant that
though his natural life was ended, his Spiritual existence
was forever. Sleep in Jesus will happen to some of us.
Death is the absence of life. Christ restored natural life to
Lazarus to show forth His power over all flesh, just as He
did for a young woman. (See Math. 4:24, 25.)

I believe that Lazarus and the maid no longer have a natural existence. When their natural life finally ended, their Spirit returned to God who gave it, waiting for the resurrection, to wit, the redemption of their bodies. When their incorruptible, glorified Spiritual body comes forth and is united with their Holy Spirit on that great resurrection morning, then they and all of God's saints will follow Christ into that place of eternal rapture. The family of God will dwell in the house of the Lord forever. Their eyes will see the King in His beauty in that land that is very far off.

Lynwood Jacobs

February 2009

HE'S COMING AGAIN

We rejoice in the promises by the prophets of His coming. We celebrate His birth. We rejoice in the words spoken during His ministry on earth. We celebrate His death, burial, and resurrection the third day. We see Him being caught up into the clouds as he departs this earth. Is that all? No. He is coming again! He is coming again to get His friends and brethren armed with the greatness of His God given power. (Matt.28:18)

Father, I will that they also, whom thou hast given me, be with me where I am, that they may behold my glory, which thou hast given me: for thou lovedst me before the foundation of the world. (John 17:24) It is evident that Christ's desire is to be with His brethren and for them to be with Him where He is now. He is alive! Thank God His Son and our Saviour is alive.

The question then becomes, who are those given unto the Son? Christ said, Father, the hour is come; glorify thy Son, that thy Son may glorify thee: As thou hast given Him power over all flesh, that He should give eternal life to as many as thou hast given Him. (See John 17:1 & 2.) The apostle Paul said moreover, whom He did predestinate, them He also called: and whom He called, them he also justified: and whom He justified, them He also glorified. (Rom. 8:31) These are the ones that were given unto Christ. They are the called, justified, and glorified of God; the Elect of God, Saints of God, Chosen of God, Perfected by Christ Jesus, the everlastingly beloved children of God.

Another question is where is Christ now? An angel told Mary at His tomb: He is not here: for He is risen. (Matt. 28:6) Christ said I will come again, and receive you unto myself; that where I am there may ye be also. (John 14:3)

He will come again and His purpose is to deliver His brethren up to ever be in the presence of God the Father, because that is where He is now. (Acts 7:56, Heb. 8:1, Mark 16:19) The Saints will behold the God-given glory of the Son of God, and the indescribable glory of God the Father in that bright land that shall never end. What a glorious hope that we will be blessed to be in that number whose names were written in heaven. (Heb. 12:23).

Christ described His coming again thusly: And then shall appear the sign of the Son of man in heaven: and then shall all the tribes of the earth mourn, and they shall see the Son of man coming in the clouds of heaven with power and great glory. (Matt. 24:30) The apostle Paul described His coming again thusly: The Lord Himself shall descend from Heaven with a shout, with the voice of the archangel, and with the Trump of God; and the dead in Christ shall rise first: Then we which are alive and remain shall be caught up together with them in the clouds, to meet the Lord in the air: and so shall we ever be with the Lord. Wherefore comfort one another with these words. (1 Thes. 4:16-18) No more comforting words than these have ever entered into my soul because they say that He is coming again for His own and I hope to be one with them.

And He shall send His angels with a great sound of a trumpet, and they shall gather together His elect from the four winds, from one end of heaven to the other. (Matt. 24:31) No matter where the Elect are at His return, whether on the highest mountain or in the utter most depths of the sea, they will come forth in His image and be gathered together, and with all the risen Family of God go home to dwell in the house of the Lord forever. (1 John 3:2 and Psalm 23:6)

Paul wrote: When Christ, who is our life, shall appear, then shall ye also appear with Him in glory. (Col. 3:4) We have no concept of the glory that shall be revealed in us at His coming if we are His. When speaking unto His Father, Christ said, "And the glory which thou gavest Me I have given them; that they may be one even as We are one." (John 17:22) There is no more joy on earth than when brethren dwell together in the unity of God's Holy Spirit of love. It is a foretaste of that life and immortality that Christ has brought to light through the gospel of peace. (2 Tim. 1:10) The purpose of this world is not for one generation to rise up, then die off and another generation come forth. The purpose of this world is to prepare the family of God for their eternal Home. When the last child of God has put on immortality and incorruption, then shall come the end and death will be swallowed up in that victory the family of God have in Jesus Christ our Lord.

For our conversation is in heaven; from whence also we look for the Saviour, the Lord Jesus Christ: Who shall change our vile body, that it may be fashioned like unto His glorious body, according to the working whereby He is able even to subdue all things unto Himself. (Phil. 3:20-21) We must have a glorified, incorruptible, immortal, spiritual body with power to ascend on high and forever be a temple of that Holy Spirit which will allow us to render praise and honor, and glory to God and to the Lamb throughout eternity. (I Cor. 15:42-44)

The following few scriptures refer to His return to receive you unto Himself that where He is there may ye may be also. There are many others:

We are looking for that blessed hope, and the glorious appearing of the Great God and our Saviour Jesus Christ. (Titus 2:13)

Behold, He cometh with Clouds; and every eye shall see Him, and they that pierced Him. (Rev. 1:7)

Henceforth there is laid up for me a crown of righteousness, which the Lord, the righteous Judge, shall give me in that day: and not me only but unto all them also that love His appearing. (II Tim. 4:8)

And when the Chief Shepherd shall appear, ye shall receive a crown of glory that fadeth not away. (I Pet. 5:4)

So Christ was once offered to bear the sins of many, and unto them that look for Him shall He appear the second time without sin unto salvation. (Heb. 9:28)

As oft as ye eat this bread and drink this cup, ye do show forth the Lord's death till He come. (I Cor. 11:26)

And when He had spoken these things, while they beheld, He was taken up; and a cloud received him out of their sight. And while they looked steadfastly toward heaven as he went up, behold, two men stood by them in white apparel; Which also said, Ye men of Galilee, why stand ye gazing up into heaven? This same Jesus, who is taken up from you into heaven, shall so come in like manner as ye have seen him go into heaven. (Acts 1: 9-11) He is coming again! Amen

Lynwood Jacobs

2007

RESURRECTION

There is one thing the Apostles never wavered on and that was the resurrection of Jesus Christ from the dead, even though they were criticized for it. They had seen the risen Christ with their own eyes as did over 500 other witnesses. The Apostle John described their experiences with the risen Christ with these words: "That which was from the beginning, which we have heard, which we have seen with our eyes, which we have looked upon, and our hands have handled of the Word of Life; (for the life was manifested and we have seen it, and bear witness, and shew unto you that eternal life, which was with the Father, and was manifested unto us;) That which we have seen and heard declare we unto you, that ye also may have fellowship with us: and truly our fellowship is with the Father, and with His Son Jesus Christ." (1 John 1: 1-3)

When the risen Christ appeared to the eleven Apostles at Jerusalem they saw him, even though at first, they were frightened and terrified. Then He told them to "Behold my hands and my feet, that it is I myself: handle me and see; for a Spirit hath not flesh and bones, as ye see me have. And when He had thus spoken, He shewed them His hands and feet. (See Luke 24: 36-40.) No wonder the Apostle John could say that their hands had handled the Word of Life. He was there before them in a body that had form and function, so surely they must have embraced Him.

The risen Christ appeared to Saul of Tarsus on the road to Damascus. Saul soon was changed by Christ from a hater of Christians to the Apostle Paul, the 12th Apostle, one of the most dedicated lovers of Christ and his Gentile brethren. So when some of the leaders of the Corinthian churches established by Paul began to deny the resurrection, Paul addressed them sternly in 1 Cor. 15:12-19. He asked, "Now if Christ be preached that He rose from the dead, how say some among you that there is no resurrection of the dead?" Paul went on to say to them that if there is no resurrection of the dead then Christ is not risen and if He is not risen, our preaching is in vain, our faith is in vain, and we are yet in our sins. Also, we have become false witnesses of God, and they which are asleep in Jesus are perished.

The preaching of the truth is never in vain, but will always accomplish that which God has ordained. There shall be a resurrection of them that are asleep in Jesus at the last day. (1 Thes.4:13-18) God-given faith worked by God-given love is never in vain but leads the Saints down the road of grace, mercy and everlasting life. (Eph.2:8-10 & John 6:29) God's people were forgiven their sins and iniquity when as yet there were none of them. (Isaiah 40:1) The children of God who are asleep in Jesus will wake up on the resurrection morning at the sound of the trumpet and the calling forth of the Son of God.

To me Christ's death and resurrection are the two most important events in the history of this world to be equaled only by the resurrection of His brethren in His image on the last day. I can understand why the world does not want to discuss this subject. It is too closely associated with death. But to those whose hope is to someday dwell in that land that is very far off, to praise, honor and glorify God and His Son, why isn't it a chief subject to be dwelt upon by them? We might say that eye hath not seen nor ear heard the things that God hath prepared for them that love Him. However, we are next told that God has revealed them unto us by His Spirit.

What has God blessed you to believe about the resurrection? Do you believe that when one dies they go to heaven or hell immediately, even Christ? At their funeral, do you believe that Mama or Daddy (or baby sister, etc) are looking down from heaven on the proceedings? Do you believe in the resurrection of the body? These are a few items that I have heard others express opinions about. Since it is the one great event that will conclude our earthly habitation, we should be able to share our hopes and beliefs about the resurrection with courtesy and love for one another. Only God and Christ know the names written in the Book of Life.

Lynwood

2010

IN HIS IMAGE

I have been asked by a beloved brother, Elder Velden Linn of Buckhannon, W. V., to express my belief about the resurrection of the body. The following is what I believe and why I believe as I do. I can only hope that it is the truth and that God Himself is the source of my belief.

I believe in the omnipotent power of Christ given Him of the Father and in the bodily resurrection of God's children in the image of Christ.

I believe that my body will be raised on that great resurrection morning with all them that are asleep in Jesus, whether in the sea, in the tomb, or scattered to the four winds.

I believe that Christ will change my vile body and fashion it like unto His glorious body that I may come forth from the tomb in His glorious image.

I believe that just as the risen Christ was the brightness of God's glory and the express image of His person so will I arise in the glorious image of Christ that I may be one with Him and all of God's children.

I believe that my raised body will be an incorruptible, glorified, spiritual body with power to ascend on high when reunited with that spiritual life force called the Holy Ghost, given me of my Father.

I believe that I have ever been a child of God, and that my pilgrimage on earth was ordained by God to perfect me for that day when I shall go HOME to that eternal inheritance that I have in Christ Jesus, that I hope is my Saviour, my Friend and beloved elder Brother.

I believe that I now have eternal life and that I may sleep in Jesus a thousand years which will be no more to me than a moment, a twinkling of an eye, when He awakens me from sleep.

I believe that I will hear that certain sound from that great trumpet that will announce His return to receive me unto Himself.

I believe that I will see Christ and all of His Holy angels when He comes to separate His sheep from the goats, and says to them on the right, "Come ye blessed of My Father, inherit the kingdom prepared for you from the foundation of the world."

I believe that I will enter Jerusalem which is above, my Spiritual mother and walk on streets of gold that are as pure glass.

I believe that I will see the nail prints in His hands and feet, and behold His riven side, and see His precious head where the crown of thorns was laid.

I believe that I will join with the family of God around that great white throne to render praises to God and to the Lamb throughout all eternity in a world without end.

When filled with the Holy Spirit, Isaiah testified to his belief in the resurrection of the dead. Thy dead men shall live, together with my dead body shall they arise. Awake and sing, ye that dwell in dust: for thy dew is as the dew of herbs, and the earth shall cast out the dead. (See Isa. 26:19.) God's children will awake from sleep and be "cast out" to come forth singing a new song filled with perfect praise unto God.

As we have born the image of the earthly, we shall also bear the image of the heavenly according to the testimony of the Apostle Paul. (I Cor. 15:49) Christ was made of a woman so he also bore the image of the earthly Adam when He was in this world. The risen Christ was the brightness of God's glory and express image of His person. We must be changed to bear the image of the heavenly Christ if we are children of God. (See Heb.1:3.)

The Apostle Paul said, "If in this life only we have hope in Christ, we are of all men most miserable." (I Cor. 15:19) In these few and simple words the Apostle expressed his belief in a life beyond the grave. He looked, as we look, for a better world where there shall be no more death, neither sorrow nor crying, neither shall there be any more pain.

Christ said to his disciples, "And this is the will of Him that sent me, that everyone who seeth the Son, and believeth on Him, may have everlasting life: And I will raise him up at the last day." (John 6:40) In this statement Christ tells us that there will be believers, and they shall be resurrected at the last day. I have seen Christ appear on the cross, and he spoke these words: "My father so loved you that he gave Me His only begotten son that you might have eternal life." After having said these words, He died before my eyes. I cannot deny my precious hope and strong belief that He is my saviour and that He will raise me up again on the last day. I know by experience that blind eyes cannot see Him and that the seeing eye is alone of the Lord.

The Apostle Paul wove together the foreknowledge and predestination of God in one powerful verse of scripture, "For whom He did foreknow, He also did predestinate to be conformed to the image of His Son, that He might be the firstborn among many brethren." (Rom. 8:29) God predestinated that His children, those He ordained unto eternal life, be conformed to the image of His son. Christ came out from God and took on Himself, not the nature of angels but the seed of Abraham, that through death He might conquer him that had the power of death. For it became Him, for whom are all things, and by whom are all things, in bringing many sons unto glory, to make the Captain of their salvation perfect through suffering. (Heb. 2:10).

Job said, "For I know that my Redeemer liveth and that He shall stand at the latter day upon the earth and though after my skin worms destroy this body, yet in my flesh shall I see God: whom I shall see for myself, and mine eyes shall behold, and not another; though my reins be consumed within me. (Job 19:25-27) I believe that Job's risen body with eyes to behold Christ when He returns will not be a natural body, but a spiritual body with power to ascend on high. Job's redeemer, righteous Abel's redeemer, and our redeemer is the same, the Son of God, Jesus Christ who is alive forevermore.

Job also asked an age old question, "If a man die shall he live again?" Job then, in effect, answered his own question. "All the days of my appointed time will I wait, till my change come. Thou shalt call, and I will answer thee: Thou wilt have a desire to the work of Thine hands." Every child of God will wait till their change comes. God must clothe them anew with incorruption and immortality because they have the victory over corruption and mortality through Christ Jesus the son of God.

Isaiah, inspired by God's spirit to speak as though he were God, said, "Fear not for I am with thee. I will bring thy seed from the east and gather thee from the west; I will say to the north, give up; and to the south keep not back: Bring

My sons from far and My daughters from the ends of the earth; Even everyone that is called by My name: for I have created him for My glory, I have formed him, yea, I have made him." (Isaiah 43:5-7) When Christ returns to receive God's people unto Himself, they will come forth from wherever they are, whether corporally alive or dead. The children of God will rise and be carried on wings of love to dwell in the house of the Lord forever. These children God created for Himself and they shall show forth His praise forever.

When speaking to his father, Christ said, "Father, I will that they also whom thou hast given Me, be with Me where I am; that they may behold My glory, which thou has given Me: For thou lovedst Me before the foundation of the world. (John 17:24) It is the will of Christ that His brethren be with Him and see Him and behold His glory, and so shall it be. We will be with Him where He is now if we be among those given to Him of the Father before the world began. Then shall we see the King in His beauty and behold the land that is very far off. What a glorious hope!

The Apostle Paul said, "For our conversation is in Heaven; from whence also we look for the Savior, the Lord Jesus Christ: Who shall change our vile body, that it may be like unto His glorious body according to the working whereby He is able to subdue all things unto Himself. (Philp. 3:20-21) I believe that Christ has all power in Heaven and in earth, even the power to change my vile body and raise my vile body and fashion it like unto His glorious body that it too may have form and function throughout the ages.

The risen Christ appeared to his disciples and said unto them, "Why are you troubled? And why do thoughts arise in your hearts? Behold my hands and feet, that it is I myself: Handle Me, and see; for a spirit hath not flesh and bones as you see Me have. (Luke 24:38-39) When Christ had thus spoken, He shewed them His hands and feet. They saw the nail prints and that His risen body had both form and function, yet, they believed not that it was He until He opened their understanding. When he saw the risen Christ and was made to understand, even doubting Thomas was made to cry out, "My Lord and my God." When God gives unto us that great Spirit of wisdom and revelation, and the eyes of our understanding is enlightened, we too will joyfully cry out, "My Lord and my God" at His appearance.

Daniel was another of the prophets of old who believed in the resurrection of the body. He said, "Many of them that sleep in the dust of the earth shall awake, some to everlasting life, and some to shame and everlasting contempt." Although we may fear that we shall awake to the shame and contempt that we deserve, we have the hope that we will awake to everlasting life by the grace and mercy of God.

Paul asked, "Now if Christ be preached that He rose from the dead, how say some among you that there is no resurrection of the dead?" Paul went on to make it plain that if there is no resurrection of the dead, then Christ is not risen. If Christ is not risen, our preaching is in vain, our faith is in vain, we are yet in our sins, we have become false witnesses of God, and they that are asleep in Jesus are perished! (See I Cor. 15:12-18.) If the dead rise not we are forever condemned to the grave and there is no reason to hope in Christ Jesus for that life and immortality that He brought to light through the gospel of peace.

Jesus, when He had cried again with a loud voice, yielded up the Ghost, and behold, the veil of the temple was rent in twain from the top to the bottom: and the earth did quake, and the rocks rent; and the graves were opened, and many bodies of the saints which slept, arose and came out of the graves after His resurrection, and went into the holy city, and appeared unto many. (Matt. 27:50-53) Strangely, this event, second only to the resurrection of Jesus Christ from the dead is not mentioned by any of the other writers of the four gospels. Here God restored natural existence to many of His children who arose from the grave with bodies that had both form and function. How astonished must have been their friends and loved ones to receive them from the grave. Oh! How great will be the rejoicing of the angels in heaven when every sinner saved by grace comes forth from mortality and rises to immortality. This scripture shows that death has no power over the Saints of God who have eternal life in Christ.

And the very God of peace sanctify you wholly; and pray God your whole spirit, and soul, and body, be preserved blameless unto the coming of our Lord Jesus Christ. (I Thes. 5:23) Christ promised to return again and receive every embodied Saint unto Himself that where He is there may they be also. He didn't promise to come receive Spirits, but the whole package, those with soul and Spirit and bodies awaiting His return.

The Apostle Paul said, "Behold, I shew you a mystery; we shall not all sleep, but we shall all be changed, in a moment, in the twinkling of an eye, at the last trump: for the trumpet shall sound, and the dead shall be raised incorruptible, and we shall be changed." (I Cor. 15:51-52) The Apostle Paul called the resurrection a mystery and the Apostle John says we will be like Him when He appears and our change comes. If we are His we shall be raised incorruptible when the trumpet sounds His return to earth. What a great hope that we will forever bear His image!

Then He said unto me, son of man, these bones are the whole house of Israel: behold, they say, our bones are dried, and our hope is lost: we are cut off for our parts. Therefore prophesy and say unto them, thus saith the Lord God; Behold, O my people, I will open your graves, and bring you into the land of Israel. And ye shall know that I am the Lord, when I have opened your graves, O my people, and brought you up out of your graves, And shall put my spirit in you, and ye shall live, and I shall place you in your own land: then shall ye know that I the Lord have spoken it, and performed it, saith the Lord. (Ezek.37:11-14) This tells us that God will bring His people out of the grave, fill them with His Spirit, and set them in their own land. Then they will know that He is not only their God but their Father. He will again fill them with His spiritual love that has bound them forever to one another, to Christ and to God.

Women received their dead raised to life again, and other saints were tortured, not accepting deliverance; that they might obtain a better resurrection. (Heb. 11:35) Elisha raised from the dead the child of a Shumanite woman. Elijah raised from the dead the son of a widow that sustained him. How blessed were those Saints of old who could not curse God and be saved. I wonder how many today would deny Him to keep from becoming a meal for hungry lions?

Christ said, "Verily, verily, I say unto you, He that heareth my word, and believeth on Him that sent Me, hath everlasting life, and shall not come into condemnation; but is passed from death unto life." (John 5:24) Who is it that heareth His word? He that is of God heareth God's word. (John 8:47) He that hears God's word believes according to the working of God's mighty power. One that believes has everlasting life and nothing can separate that one from the love of God that is in Christ Jesus our Lord. That one has been resurrected from a first death in trespasses and in sin to a newness of life in Christ. Over them the second death hath no power.

The Apostle Paul described the resurrection of the dead as follows: "It is sown in corruption; it is raised in incorruption. It is sown in dishonor; it is raised in glory. It is sown in weakness; it is raised in power. It is sown a natural body; raised a spiritual body. There is a natural body, and there is a spiritual body…As we have borne the image of the earthy, we shall also bear the image of the heavenly…We shall not all sleep; but we shall all be changed, in a moment, in the twinkling of an eye; the trumpet shall sound, and the dead shall be raised incorruptible." (I Cor. 15:42-44, 49-52) The same "it" that is sown in corruption is the same "it" that is raised incorruptible!

Christ said, "Verily, verily, I say unto you, the hour is coming, and now is, when the dead shall hear the voice of the Son of God, and they that hear shall live." (John 5:25) Did not Lazarus, who was "dead" hear the voice of the Son of God and lived? All of God's children will hear the voice of the Son of God on the resurrection morn because they are dead in Christ, yeah, asleep in Jesus, and they shall arise and live forevermore. Now, in this life, they receive a hearing ear and seeing eye that they may know in part, but then they shall see as they are seen and know as they are known.

Jesus told Martha, "I am the resurrection, and the life: he that believeth on me, though he were dead, yet shall he live: And whosoever liveth and believeth in me shall never die. Believeth thou this? (John 11:25-26) They may be dead in sin, but this will not prevent God's spirit from instilling life into His chosen generation, (not choosing generation). At the appointed time of the Father, they will be born again of an incorruptible spirit. This spirit is an eternal life force that belongs eternally to those who receive it, though it may return to God who gave it to await those words of Christ to our dead bodies that mean, "Live, arise and manifest the fruits of a Holy Spirit that will forever replace mortal blood in your living body."

Christ said, "Marvel not at this: for the hour is coming, in the which all that are in the graves shall hear His voice, And shall come forth; they that have done good, unto the resurrection of life; and they that have done evil, unto the resurrection of damnation." (John 5:25-29) Even the Pharisees believed in the resurrection of both the just and the unjust. The apostle John saw the dead, small and great, stand before God. He saw those whose names were not written in the Book of Life judged according to their (dead) works. All were cast into the lake of fire except those whose names were found written in the Book of Life. Those saints were judged according to the work of God, because it is the work of God that we believe on Jesus Christ. Those saints were judged according to the finished work of Christ who died for their sins once in the end of the world.

Paul said, "But I would not have you to be ignorant, brethren, concerning them which are asleep, that ye sorrow not, even as others which have no hope." (I Thes. 5:14) When the God of hope fills us with all joy and peace in believing, then we may abound in hope through the power of His Holy Spirit. Then we sorrow not, but are made to accept His will in all things.

Paul added, "For if we believe that Jesus died and arose again, even so them also which sleep in Jesus will God bring with Him." (I The. 5-14) Christ is going to return, according to His promise and receive His people unto Himself that where He is there they may be also. The family of God will rise as one to meet the Lord in the air. (See John 17:24.)

Paul finished by saying, "For the Lord Himself shall descend from heaven with a shout, with the voice of the archangel, and with the trump of God: and the dead in Christ shall rise first: Then we which are alive and remain shall be caught up together with them in the clouds to meet the Lord in the air: and so shall we ever be with the Lord." (I Thes. 5:16-17) What a glorious hope! As many as were ordained unto eternal life will go home to that city with foundation whose builder and maker is God.

The above scriptures coming through the Prophets and Apostles and above all from Christ Jesus Himself lend support to my belief and strengthen my hope that I will come forth from the grave with a body that has both form and function as a temple for my everlasting Spirit, and that I will arise in the image of my precious Saviour and bask in His God given righteousness, and joy, and peace forever.

Lynwood Jacobs

August 2002

JOHN 17

John 17 is the most unique chapter in the Bible, to me. It is the only chapter devoted totally to Christ speaking directly to His Father. Because of this, as a source of sound doctrine there is none to equal it. Election, eternal life, grace, eternal unity of Christ and the church, God's love and omnipotence, true witnessing, Glory of God, Christ's finished work and desire to ever be with His brethren--all are brought forth by Christ in love and simplicity.

No one can read John 17:1, 2 with understanding and deny the doctrine of election. They read, "These words spake Jesus, and lifted up his eyes to heaven, and said, Father the hour is come; glorify thy Son, that thy Son also may glorify thee: As thou hast given him power over all flesh, that he should give eternal life to as many as thou hast given him." I believe that when Christ lifted up His eyes, He was looking into heaven itself, and seeing God as He talked directly to His Father on high. The gift of eternal life and the electing grace of God are here declared, and the saving grace in Christ Jesus which was soon to be made manifest. When Jesus had spoken the last words to His Father as recorded in John 17, he went forth with his disciples to be crucified. Yes, Christ's hour had come to die on the cross as a sin sacrifice, and to rise again to show the power of God over all flesh, a power that God had given his Son in the beginning, that his Son should give eternal life to His brethren, and none others.

"I pray for them: I pray not for the world, but for them which thou hast given me; for they are thine. And all mine are thine, and thine are mine; and I am glorified in them. Neither pray I for these alone, but them also which shall believe on me through their word." (John 17:9, 10, 20)

What a glorious oneness of the Father and Son with those whose names are in the Book of Life. This is more conformation of the eternal unity of Christ and the Church. If we are His now, we have ever been His. Christ also testified here that God sends His own chosen vessels into the world to declare the TRUTH to His believing children. The TRUTH brings to remembrance the things that be of God and Christ, that have been revealed to His children by the Holy Spirit. God has had from the beginning a few upon this earth that worship Him. (See Gen .4:24.) It has ever been the Spirit that enlightened this remnant according to the election of grace.

"O righteous Father, the world hath not known thee: but I have known thee, and these have known that thou hast sent me. And I have declared unto them thy name, and will declare it: that the love wherewith thou hast loved me may be in them, and I in them." (John 17:25, 26) The world may hear about God, but their claim to know Him by natural means is false. The love of God in Christ is the same everlasting love that comes as a gift to a child of God at the appointed time of the Father. It is called the Comforter, and makes manifest "Christ in you the hope of Glory."

"Father, I will that they also, whom thou hast given me, be with me where I am; that they behold my glory, which thou has given me; for thou lovedst me before the foundation of the world." (John 17:24) More glorious words! Christ's will is to have His brethren with Him where He is now, that they might behold Him, the glorified Son of God. Where is He? He is now at the right hand of the Father, so that when His brethren see Him again they will also be in the everlasting presence of the Holiest of the Holy, almighty

God. If blessed, we will be in that number that Christ promised to raise again and glorify at the last day.

"I have glorified thee on the earth; I have finished the work which thou gravest me to do." (John 17:4) Some maintain that Christ only half finished the work that God gave Him to do, but that man has to do His part for it to be a finished work. The finished work that Christ did on earth was afore ordained to glorify His Father. It did just that, and to perfection. A part of that work was the perfecting of the Saints of God, something they could not do for themselves, then or now. Because of His work He hath perfected forever them that are sanctified, them that were chosen and set apart in Him before the foundation of the world.

God has blessed me to enjoy reading of the simplicity in Christ Jesus that is so rightly described in John 17. May you enjoy it as well.

Lynwood Jacobs

May 2011

HEAR

Three similar scriptures in the 5th chapter of John stress the absolute need to hear. To me, the first verse is the promise from God, the second is the promise fulfilled on earth, and the third is the promise renewed forever. In each verse Christ said we must be blessed to hear. To understand what we hear, we need a spiritual ear.

The Promise: "Verily, verily, I say unto you, he that heareth my word, and believeth on Him that sent me, hath everlasting life, and shall not come into condemnation; but is passed from death unto life." (John 5:24)

The Promise Fulfilled: "Verily, verily, I say unto you, the hour is coming, and now is, when the dead shall hear the voice of the Son of God; and they that hear shall live." (John 5:25)

The Promise Renewed Forever: "Marvel not at this: for the hour is coming, in the which all that are in the grave shall hear His voice, and shall come forth; they that have done good unto the resurrection of life; and they that have done evil, unto the resurrection of damnation." (John 5:28,29)

The hearing ear and the seeing eye, the Lord hath made them both. (Prov. 20:12) Unless God gives us the ability, we cannot hear and have Spiritual understanding of Christ's words in these three scriptures. "He that is of God heareth God's word." (John 8:47) Though God has created us, and given us this earthly tabernacle for our use on earth, its ear cannot hear. We must be born again, born of the Spirit, born of God, to hear with understanding the things that are freely given us of God. Two of His greatest gifts are Christ, who gave us the words of truth, and a Spiritual ear that we might hear and understand His words of truth.

"Howbeit, many of them which heard the word believed; and the number of them was about five thousand." (Acts 4:4) This is a great number of manifest believers, saints of God, who were ordained unto eternal life by God. (See Acts 13:48.) What did they hear and believe? They heard Peter and others preach through Jesus the resurrection of the dead, the same thing that Christ preached in the three scriptures under consideration here.

Why do I believe that John 5:24 was the promise of God? Because it says that we must not only hear Christ's words, but we must believe in God who sent Him. We must believe that God is the one who ordained eternal life for His children through Christ before the world began. We must believe it is God who chose His children in Christ before the world began. We must know the love God had for His children even before any of them were manifest in the world. It is God who made an everlasting covenant with His Son who would come and redeem His brethren from their sins, and free them from condemnation. It is God that ordained His children be born of the Spirit as part of the perfecting of the Saints for their eternal home.

Why do I believe that John 5:25 is the manifestation of the promise in John 5:24? Christ said the hour is coming, and now is, when the dead shall hear His voice. Time applies to this. Ever since time began, these words apply to those dead in sin who have been born again, and called out of nature's darkness into the marvelous light of the Son of God. These are the ones whose names are written in the Book of Life, and I believe the first names therein are Adam and Eve. When born again, God's children are alive forevermore. Yeah, though they sleep thousands of years they will awaken on that last day that Christ speaks about in John 5:28, 29 when there will be no more time.

Christ said marvel not at the first two scriptures. Why? He is coming again, the graves will be opened, and all will hear His voice. He will say to the ones on His right, "Come ye blessed of my Father, inherit the Kingdom prepared for you from the foundation of the world." They will arise in His likeness. He will then deliver up the kingdom unto God. His work will be finished, and He will then lay down all God given power and rule that God may once again be all in all. What a glorious day that will be! I hope to be there with those on the right.

Lynwood Jacobs

January 2011

HOPE

Now the God of hope fill you with all joy and peace in believing, that ye may abound in hope, through the power of the Holy Ghost. (Rom. 15:15) What joy and peace fills the souls of Saints who have been born of God, filled with hope, and made to believe according to the workings of His mighty Spirit. (See Eph. 1:19.) Faith, hope, and charity, these three, but the greatest of these is charity. (See I Cor. 13:13.) God's love in us works our God given faith, and our faith gives substance to the things we hope for. (See Heb. 11:1 and Gal. 5:6.)

In nature, hope looks only forward! In the Spirit, hope looks not only forward, but also looks to the past and the present. What are some of the things God's children hope for? Through the Spirit, they hope that God chose them in Christ Jesus before the world began, and wrote their name in the Book of Life. (See Eph. 1:4 and Rev. 20:15.) They hope for that eternal life which God who cannot lie, promised in Christ Jesus before the world began. (See Titus 1:2.)

They hope that they have been born again of the Spirit, yea, that they have been born of God! They hope for a thankful heart that they may ever be thankful to God from whom all blessings flow. (See James 1:17.) They hope that God will forever reconcile them to His will as He did for His Son near the end of Christ's sojourn on earth. (See Mark 14:35, 36.) Also, they hope that they have Christ in them the hope of glory, for He is their hope. Above all else, they thank God for their hope that Christ died to take away their sins, and that He has promised to return and carry His brethren home to be where He is now. (See John 14:1-4.)

The writer of the Book of Hebrews described what hope means to the child of God, saying it is an anchor of the soul, both sure and steadfast. The writer said that the law made nothing perfect but the bringing in of a better HOPE did; by the which we draw nigh unto God. (See Heb. 7:19.) The children of God have a desire, that through the new birth, a strong faith, and a lively hope, they may regain that closeness to God that their parents lost in the Garden of Eden.

The psalmist said, "Thou art my hope, O Lord." (Psa. 71:5) Titus looked for the Blessed Hope and Glorious Appearing of our Lord and Saviour Jesus Christ. (See Tit. 2:13.) Peter hoped to the end. Paul rejoiced in hope. Solomon said the Righteous have Hope in His death. (See Prov. 14:3.)

I believe that a Spirit of wisdom and revelation in the knowledge of God has taught me that when it comes to God and Godliness, without that Spirit, I know nothing as I ought. By that same Spirit, I believe I have been given a blessed hope, that I might praise God, and rejoice in Christ Jesus forever. God does not need me, I need God. I cannot atone for my sins--Christ atoned for all the sins of His brethren. I believe that He has blessed me with a Spirit of repentance from dead works to serve the LIVING God. The Father, the Son, and the Holy Ghost, these three are my Hope.

Lynwood Jacobs

March 2008

WISH, WANT, WILL

<u>Strong's Exhaustive Concordance of the King James Version of the Bible</u> does not show one instance of God wishing, or of God wanting. It does have many pages in reference to God's will. One newer version of the Bible reverses the above. An example: in KJV it is recorded, "The king's heart is in the hand of the Lord, as the rivers of water: he turneth it whithersoever he will." (Prov. 21:1) In a new version that someone gave me, it says about the same thing, but the last words, <u>He wishes,</u> is substituted for <u>He will.</u> The thought I had when I read this was: Now they've got their god right where they want him. He does the wishing and wanting, and they do the willing. How disgusting! I no longer have that copy of the new version. The KJV version is said to be 400 years old this year. If it was good enough for my grandfather, and 2 great grandfathers, all gifted Elders in the Hardshell Primitive Baptist Church, it is good enough for me.

God ordained every minute detail to make manifest all events in time and space that He willed to come to pass. He even ordained that which is not, to bring to naught that which is, that no flesh should glory in His presence. According to His will He raises up, and brings down. He gives life and takes away life, both at the ordained time determined by His will before the world was. Those who say God wishes and wants know absolutely nothing about the Creator of this Universe, and certainly have not been born again of His Spirit. Many were ordained by God to substitute the word of man for the good word of God, and they have not been given to hope in the finished work of Jesus Christ.

Christ came to do the will of God, not the wishes or wants of God. In John 17:24 Christ also expressed His will, but I'm assured that it was in no way contrary to the will of God, "Father, I will that they also, whom thou hast given me, be with me where I am; that they may behold my glory, which thou hast given me: for thou lovedst me before the foundation of the world." What a great hope we have when blessed with a strong desire to be one with those given to Christ by His Father. At the ordained time of the will of God, they will be with Christ where He is now, and behold His glory as the only begotten Son of God.

Lynwood Jacobs

October 2011

BAPTISMS

When I try to describe the indescribable or explain the imponderable with man's words, I hope to wind up telling the truth. Recognizing this established my need to preface my remarks with –"I believe, or I don't believe." If what I have been given to believe is the truth, it needs no defending, and if it is a lie, it can't be defended. This is my belief about baptisms:

The writer of the book of Hebrews actually said that one of the foundation principles of the doctrine of Christ was the doctrine of baptisms (Heb. 6:2). There are two distinct baptisms mentioned in the Bible. I believe they are the ones that apply here. They are the baptism of Christ (Matt. 3:11) and the baptism of John (Luke 20:4). They are totally different in purpose, substance, and effect.

Simply stated, John's baptism is a baptism of hope, while Christ's baptism is a baptism of hope fulfilled. Baptism in water by man does not save a soul. Baptism of the Holy Spirit by Christ saves a soul. Christ's baptism comes first, or John's baptism is a waste of time. John's baptism does not reveal the things that are of God. Christ's baptism reveals the things that are of God.

If blessed, let us first go to the bank of the river Jordan where John is baptizing believers. A man called Jesus comes to be baptized, but as he steps into the water John tries to forbid him, saying, "I have need to be baptized of thee." The man called Jesus tells John, "Suffer it to be so now: for thus it becometh us to fulfill all righteousness." We see John then immerse Jesus in the river Jordan. As Jesus comes up out of the water a marvelous thing occurs. The heavens open up and the Spirit of God like a dove lights upon Jesus, and a voice from heaven says, "This is my beloved Son, in whom I am well pleased." Overwhelmed, those of us standing there on the bank of the river Jordan are left to ponder, what does all this mean?

The above makes one wonder, who was this man called John who was the first, as far as we know, to baptize in the name of the Father, the Son and the Holy Ghost? Surely the crowning event of his life was to baptize Christ in the river Jordan. It will be interesting to learn more about him to help us with the question, what hath God wrought?

John's appearance was foreordained of God to prepare the way of the Lord (Isa. 40:3-5, Luke 3:4). He was a preacher. (Matt. 3:1). He preached baptism of repentance for the remission of sins. (Luke 3:3) He baptized those who confessed their sins. (Matt. 3:6) He did not baptize all that came to him, but sent many away to bring forth fruits meet for repentance.(Matt. 3:8) His statement of his purpose was, "I indeed baptize you with water unto repentance: but He that cometh after me is mightier than I, whose shoes I am not worthy to bear: He shall baptize you with the holy ghost and with fire:" (Matt. 3:11) The dove from above assured John that Jesus was the promised Lamb of God who came into the world to take away sin. (John 1:29&34) He knew that he needed to be baptized of Him. To summarize: John was a preacher sent forth by God to publicly immerse believers unto repentance for the remission of their confessed sins. Today, as then, those who immerse, and those who are immersed must believe that Jesus Christ is the beloved Son of God. They that truly believe that Jesus Christ is the son of God are born of God. One of the first things a manifested child of God learns is their need to confess and be forgiven for their sins. So John was baptizing those who were ordained unto eternal life, those who had already been baptized by the Holy Spirit.

Remittance of sin here means the transmittance of sin from the sinner to Christ. Remission of sin means forgiveness of sin for the elect that Christ died for. The psalmist David said, "Blessed is he whose transgression is forgiven, whose sin is covered. Blessed is the man unto whom the Lord imputeth not iniquity, and in whose spirit there is no guile." The Apostle Paul speaking of the same thing said, "Even as David also describeth the blessedness of the man unto whom God imputeth righteousness without works, Saying, Blessed are they whose iniquities are forgiven, and whose sins are covered. Blessed is the man to whom God will not impute sin. (Rom. 4:6-8) These blessed of God are those He chose in Christ before the world began, the very elect of God. They are those whose sins were imputed to Christ before the world began in an everlasting covenant of promise he made with His Father. It was a promise that Christ would die for his brethren on Calvary to fulfill that promise that He would put their sins as far away as the east is from the west.

John said, "Christ shall baptize you with the Holy Ghost, and with fire." Christ's baptism makes one a manifested child of God for it is one with the new birth. It must come first or John's baptism is nothing more than an empty gesture. Christ's baptism is for those who were ordained unto eternal life, those who are made to believe according to the workings of God's mighty power, those children of promise called out of nature's darkness by the gift of the Holy Spirit. Christ's baptism is a consuming fire that soon destroys self-righteousness, trust in man, free-willism, hatred, judgment, legalism, head knowledge, and any other confidence in the flesh.

What are some of the differences between the two Baptisms? One is temporal; the other is eternal. One is natural; the other is Spiritual. One is a hope of immortality; the other is a gift of immortality. One is a confession of faith; the other is a gift of faith. One is administered by man; the other is administered by Christ. One may gain access to the visible church; the other gives access to the general assembly and church of the first born which are written in heaven. (Heb. 12:23) Is John's baptism sufficient unto itself to save a soul? No. Only Christ's baptism can be sufficient unto itself to save a soul. Examples of the latter are King David and the thief on the cross, both confessed sinners. Water baptism is a public confession that one is a sinner and that one believes that Jesus Christ is the son of God who came to take away sin. It is for those whose souls have been saved.

Lynwood Jacobs

2010

PRAISE

Written words that praise and honor God and Christ are called doxologies. In a marvelous Book of mysteries called Revelation, the Apostle John was blessed through the Spirit to give many examples of these words of praise, spoken by a great diversity of glorifiers. In one example, four and twenty elders declared, "Thou art worthy, O Lord, to receive glory and honor and power: for thou hast created all things, and for thy pleasure they are and were created." (Rev. 4:11) These words, spoken by elders who were in the very presence of God, not only praise Him, but also are words of revelation to the Church. They state simply that God is the creator of all things, and that He has created all things for His pleasure. That is why He created both vessels of wrath and vessels of mercy. That is why He created the elect and non-elect. That is why He ordained both natural death, and Spiritual life. It is God's good pleasure for all events in time and eternity to come to pass because of the perfection of HIS will.

As I lay in bed last night the power and pleasure of God mentioned in the above scripture came to mind. Then a man appeared before my eyes as he looked upward and said," Lord, I'm going to spend the day with you." The Lord answered and said, "Very well, my son." Immediately the sky darkened and a great tornado destroyed the man's house. He was able to survive by diving into the cellar. As he came up the dark clouds began to rain in sheets. Before he reached dry ground he was up to his waist in water. As he lay near exhaustion, an enormous roar told him that water was rushing down the valley, because a great earthquake had destroyed the dam. By a huge effort the man was able to get to higher ground. At the end of the day, thankful to be alive, the man looked up and asked the Lord, "Why?" God answered him," Because, my son, it was my pleasure to show you who has all power."

Another example of a doxology occurred when John heard a great host of angels and beasts and elders say with a loud voice, "… Worthy is the lamb that was slain to receive power, and riches, and wisdom, and strength, and honour, and glory, and blessing." (Rev. 5:11, 12) The Lamb of God, Jesus Christ, was worthy to receive all these things from God after he was slain, and rose again to perfect forever them that are sanctified. (Heb.10: 10,14) He rose from the grave with all power in heaven and in earth. (Matt. 28:18) The Lamb has power over all flesh to give eternal life to as many as His Father has given Him. (John 17:2) The riches of His grace shine upon, and keep His friends while they are in this world. (John 17:24) He glorified His Father on earth as His Father glorified Him. Through the power of the Comforter given by Christ, His brethren are blessed to worship Him to whom be glory both now and forever.(John 16:7) What a wonderful Saviour!

Lynwood Jacobs

2011

WORKS

In his letter to the saints at Ephesus (and to all saints today, and I hope to be one), the Apostle Paul reveals the source of good works: "For by grace are you saved through faith; and that not of yourselves: it is the gift of God: Not of works, lest any man should boast. For we are His workmanship, created in Christ Jesus unto good works, which God hath before ordained that we should walk in them." (Eph.2:8-10) Grace is a divine attribute of God by which His children are gifted with undeserved blessings. Faith is a gift of God. With God's gift of His love in our heart, our holy faith then worketh by love to give real substance to the things we hope for. A blessed hope in Christ is an anchor to our soul, both sure and steadfast, that will never let us be ashamed of Him, even unto death. His Spirit in us frees us from dead works to serve the living God.

If we are what we hope to be, we are God's workmanship. He purposed us in Christ Jesus when He chose us in Him before the world was and ordained that we would be manifest in this time world to prepare us for our everlasting home with Them. God before ordained that when we were born again of the Holy Spirit, we would manifest the fruits of this Spirit. With the love of God shed abroad in our heart, we will walk in that path of righteousness that leadeth unto life everlasting. God's love is the most powerful force in this world. It leads the children of God to manifest the good works before ordained of God that they should walk in them. IT IS THE HOLY SPIRIT THAT DIRECTS US TO DO GOOD WORKS, not the other way around. When WE think WE did a good work, WE didn't.

I hope that God will reconcile us to the fact that we do His will while here on earth, just as did His precious Son and our saviour, Jesus Christ. We can then hope that our prayers are true thankfulness to our heavenly Father for His electing grace, manifested mercy, and loving kindness. Though we may have had tribulations, and periods of darkness, yet, we can rejoice in Christ our Light and be truly thankful to Him for His great suffering, that we might have everlasting life. We can worship together with our beloved brethren in peace, and in truth, no more acting at times as though the church is little more than a court of law. We will continue to be able to speak, or write what we believe about spiritual things. If it is the truth, it needs no defending. If not the truth, it can't be defended.

Lynwood Jacobs

August 2011

GOD IS SUPREME

This is written by one, and for those, that I hope worships the one only living and true God who is before all things and by whom all things consist. He is God and hath made this world and all things therein. He is Lord of heaven and of earth, and hath created all things for His pleasure, whether they be in heaven or in earth, whether they be visible or invisible, whether they be thrones, dominions, principalities or powers. To me that means that this world and all therein are the perfect creation of God for the purpose that He has in them! He is the rock, His work is perfect! (See Deut. 32:4.) I have made the earth and created man upon it: I, even my hands have stretched out the heavens, and all their host have I commanded. (Isa. 45:12)

To try to understand our God through feeble sense alone is folly. If God has ordained for one to walk in darkness and have no light that one will walk in darkness. If God has ordained for one to walk in the light, God will make the light to shine out of darkness and that one will walk in the light. It is the Lord that flips the ON switch, not man. (See 2 Sam. 22:29; Job 29:2-3; Psa.27:1.)

I don't believe this world is here for one generation to live and die off just to be replaced by another generation to live and die off. I believe that this world has two main purposes. One, it was a place for Jesus Christ to come down to earth to learn obedience and make His bride perfect by the things He suffered. Two, it is a place for God to bring forth His children one by one and prepare them for the world to come. It is called the perfecting of the Saints. (See Eph.4th Chapter.) When the last little child of God has been born again and fully prepared for that home on high, there will be no further need for this world. Christ will return and call forth His brethren and carry them home to dwell in the house of the Lord forever. (See John 14:1-4 and Rev. 21:1-5.)

For He bringeth down them that dwell on high; the lofty city, He layeth it low; He bringeth it even to the dust. The foot shall tread it down, even the feet of the poor, and the steps of the needy. (Isa. 26: 5,6) On 9/11 God showed forth His power again to His children by bringing down two tall buildings with the inhabitants therein whose time had come to die. (See Eccl.3: 1, 2.) In 1945 using the ordained genius of Einstein and the Enola Gay and Bachscar, He destroyed two Japanese cities. Poof! They were gone. During WWII, He brought down other great cities to the dust to show forth His power and make His name to be called upon for mercy and deliverance. Ancient cities, such as Sodom and Gomorrah, and Empires are no more, having been brought low by God, and the feet of the poor and needy walk thereon. He has brought forth plagues as he did to the Egyptians to show forth His power and make His name known throughout the earth. Are we any better than those who have known the wrath of God, or will our great cities know it again? (Rom.9:22-24, Eph. 2:3, 1Thes.1:10, Rom. 1:18-20, Psalms 78:31-33)

Thou hast set our iniquities before thee, our secret sins in the light of thy countenance. For all our days are passed away in thy wrath; we spend our years as a tale that is told. (Psalms 90:8, 9) God afore ordained that every human would come forth on earth sinners by nature. (See Rom.3:23, Gal.3:22.) God afore ordained that the elects sins and iniquities would be imputed to Christ and that God's righteousness would be imputed to the elect through Christ. (See 2 Cor. 5:21) God's righteousness is the only righteousness acceptable to Him. If we walk in the way that leads unto life everlasting, it is because God's Spirit has directed our steps on that path. If we walk in the way that leads unto destruction, it is because God has NOT ordained for us to walk on paths of righteousness for His names sake. (See Prov. 16:9.) God's children don't accept Christ, they were made accepted unto to God in the Beloved. (See Eph.1:5, 6.) Lord, thou wilt ordain peace for us: for thou hast wrought all our works in us. (Isa. 26:12) Trust in the Lord with all thine heart; and lean not unto thine own understanding. In all thy ways acknowledge Him, and He shall direct thy paths. (Prov. 3:5, 6)

But God has chosen the foolish things of the world to confound the wise; and God hath chosen the weak things of the world to confound the things that are mighty; and base things of the world, and things which are despised hath God chosen, yea, and things which are not to bring to nought the things that are: That no flesh should glory in His presence. (1 Cor.1:27-29) Not many wise men after the flesh are called. Solomon, said by some to be the wisest man who ever lived, in his latter days followed after the gods of his wives. Worldly wisdom is not enough. (See 1 Cor. 1:26.) There is nothing more foolish to the world than the preaching of the cross. (See 1 Cor. 1:23.) There is no greater weakness to the world than to turn the other cheek, or to love your enemies.

Many today would not fellowship King David, who though a murderer and adulterer, was a man after God's own heart. Many say to believe in someone that can't be seen is madness. Christ told Thomas that blessed are they who haven't seen Me, or put their hand into the nail prints, or into My riven side, yet believe that I am the Son of God. (See John 20:29.) There are those that believe that baptism in the water of this world by man replaces baptism of the Holy Ghost in the River of Life by the High Priest. Water baptism has meaning only when it is in conjunction with true baptism which is baptism with the Holy Ghost and with fire. (Matt.3:11, Luke 3:16, Acts 1:5)

I form the light, and create darkness: I make peace and create evil: I the lord do all these things. (Isa. 45:7) Spiritual darkness is the absence of Spiritual light. Only God can make the Light to shine out of darkness. (See 2 Cor. 4:6.) True peace is a gift of God and belongs only to those that God ordained to be reconciled to His will.

God said that he created evil and I am not going to call Him a liar as long as I am in my present mind. God has created all things for Himself: yea, even the wicked for the day of evil. (See Proverbs 16:4.) I believe that God created evil when, with His own hand, He formed the crooked serpent. (See Job 26:13.) God ordained that man would be tempted of evil from the beginning or temptation would not have occurred. The Truth does not tempt. (See James 1:13-15.) It takes a liar to lie and tempt. No part of the triune Godhead could lie or tempt with evil so with His own hand God formed the crooked serpent, which has lied and tempted from the beginning. The serpent told Eve that God was a liar, and the old devil has been testifying to such lies ever since. Eve's actions and Adams reaction were ordained of God or they could have eaten of the Tree of Life, which was there in the Garden, and lived forever. Then we would not be here. (See Gen.3:1-4.) The result is that they that are in the flesh cannot please God, which makes manifest every child of Gods need for a new birth, and the predetermined saving grace in the Lord and Saviour Jesus Christ. From personal experience, I know the same evil Spirit from the Lord that entered into the mouth of Ahab's prophets. From a greater experience, I believe that I have received a blessed Spirit that has given me a lively hope that I have been delivered into the family of God.

Thine, O Lord, is the greatness, and the power, and the victory, and the majesty: for all that is in heaven and in the earth is thine: Thine is the kingdom, O Lord, and Thou art exalted as head above all. (1 Chron. 29:11)

Lynwood Jacobs

January 2009

PRAYER

I create the fruit of the lips: Peace, peace to him that is far off, and to him that is near, sayeth the Lord, and I will heal him. (Isa. 57:19) The fruit of the lips that pray to God are wrought by God. They come after His peace has been established in a troubled mind, and after the balm of His love has healed a sin sick soul.

By Him therefore let us offer the sacrifice of praise to God continually, that is, the fruit of our lips giving thanks to His name. (Heb. 13:15) The fruit of the lips from a prayerful heart are the spiritual sacrifices of praise to God that are not vain repetition. The central themes of a true prayer are, "I thank thee, O Father, Lord of heaven and of earth" and "Not my will, but Thine be done," and "Thine is the Kingdom, and the power, and the glory forever, amen." (See Matt. 6:9-13.) Asking God for more than forgiveness or our daily bread is apt to be begging, and not praying, which is thankfulness to Him for what we have. God knows our thoughts from afar off, whether they be good or evil, and is acquainted with all our ways. He is able to do exceeding abundantly above all that we ask or think. (See Eph. 3:20, 21; Heb. 4:12; Psalm 94:11; Luke 6:.8.)

In a circular letter in 1881 Elder Bill Perkins of south Louisiana wrote, "Prayer must come in, by, and through the Holy Spirit. So we thank God in prayer because His Spirit is there to indict our hearts to thankfulness, to praise, to honor, to glorify, yea, to worship Him in Spirit and in Truth." In the Spirit we are thankful, not only for our blessings, but for our trials and tribulations, also. Why? For tribulations worketh patience, and patience, experience, and experience, hope, And hope maketh not ashamed because the love of God is shed abroad in our hearts by the

Holy Ghost which is given us of God. (See Rom. 5:3-5.) Trials and tribulation are a part of that process called the perfecting of the Saints. (See John 16:33.)

The most beautiful prayer I ever heard came from the lips of an aged Brother whose wife was taken from him the day after their 70th wedding anniversary. As we stood by her casket at the funeral home, I heard him softly say, "Thank you, Lord, for giving me Pearl." I knew then that Brother Charlie would be all right. A thankful heart for what God had given him had eased the great pain at what God had taken from him.

Lynwood Jacobs

1975 and 2009

GOD'S SOVEREIGNTY

Many years ago I read the following amazing statement about the Sovereignty of God from the "Bible Handbook" by Henry H. Halley, p. 527. "How to reconcile the Sovereignty of God and the Freedom of the Human Will we do not know. Both doctrines are plainly taught in the Bible. But to explain how both can be true, we shall have to leave to others." My first thought was that it is impossible to reconcile the Sovereignty of God and the free will or free moral agency of man. My second thought was, and still is, to thank God for not hanging me on the horns of that dilemma. Many that are smarter than I am have tried and failed.

I have been given a simple but profound belief that the Lord God Omnipotent reignith. His will is done in heaven and on earth. This is contrary to those who say man wills and God wishes and wants. My hope is that God will turn their world upside down and reveal to them that God willed and man wishes and wants. To say that God wants, or would if you will let Him, or that He wishes you would accept Christ is an abomination! If my God "wanted" me to do something and I wouldn't do it and He couldn't do anything about it says that He is nothing more than one of the gods many and gods plenty abroad in the land. I believe that He is the one only living and true God—supreme, omnipotent, before all things and by whom all things consist. He is certainly not the weak, begging, undone being so often presented in print and from the pulpits of the world.

I believe that God created the universe and made our world and all things therein. I believe that He planted a garden eastward in Eden and created two vessels of mercy afore prepared unto glory and placed them in the garden. Some seem to suggest that God then turned his back, crossed His fingers, and wondered what Adam and Eve would do next. How utterly ridiculous! God had ordained every step they would take, every condition they would undergo, every situation they would face, every act they would perform, and every thought that would direct their lives. This is that doctrine of absolute predestination that not only pertained to Adam and Eve but pertains to all people and all events in time and eternity.

God ordained that temptation would appear in the Garden of Eden or it would not have taken place. God is Truth and Truth cannot tempt. It takes a lie to tempt, so He whose Spirit garnished the heavens, with His own hands formed the crooked serpent to lie and tempt. Adam and Eve had no power to resist temptation. If so, they would have eaten of the tree of life and have lived forever. Then there would have been no need for the blessed Son of God to come down from God and learn obedience by the things He suffered. An everlasting covenant between the Father and His Son would have been annulled and come to naught. There would be no resurrection of the dead because there never would have been anyone to die. God is the Rock. His work is perfect. God has a holy and divine purpose in all events that come to pass. As sin laden as we feel to be, each one of us is the perfect creation of a perfect God for the purpose that He has in us. Adam was the first created son of God who had a holy and divine purpose in creating Adam weak in the flesh. God had chosen His family in Christ, imputed their every sin to Christ; and imputed His righteousness to each one of His children through Christ before He formed Adam from the dust of the earth. Adam needed the electing grace of God and the saving grace in Christ Jesus the same as we do today. God created Adam subject to vanity, not willingly but by reason of God who subjected Adam in hope. Vanity here means an absence of the Spirit. When Adam and Eve were born again of an incorruptible Seed, they received the Spirit to help with those itchy fig leaves of their own self-righteousness. Adam received that Spirit of wisdom and revelation and the eyes of his understanding were enlightened that Adam might know the riches of God's grace in His kindness toward His children through Jesus Christ. Adam, Eve, and righteous Abel had the same hope of eternal life in Christ Jesus that their brothers and sisters have in this day.

Much of the following is excerpted from a letter written by me in December 1972. Thirty plus years later, I still hope and believe it is the doctrine of God and of Christ Jesus.

The Doctrine of Absolute Predestination was given to His children by an absolute God. It was not given to the world. This doctrine is called Fatalism by a pseudo-religious world who knows not God, so they have substituted a vague term "fate" that is about as elusive as their begging, blind, and unsettled god. There are those who say God predestinated the good things, such as eternal life, but none of the bad things. This group is the most perplexing of all to me, and here is why. If a man believes in the absolute sovereignty of God, I know where he stands. If a man believes in the doctrine of the free will of man, I know where he stands. But when one tries to mix the two, he is trying to pawn off on me a half-sheep, half-goat, half-elect, half-non-elect, half-works, half-grace, part this part that, mish-mash that would confuse the devil himself if it wasn't for the fact that such is the devil's doctrine.

God is God, blessed forevermore. He only has all the divine attributes of Himself. He is sovereign, everlasting, omnipotent, all wise, gracious and loving toward His children, and these are only parts of His ways. To me, this is what the Doctrine of Absolute Predestination tells the church. His attributes are unchangeable and Spiritual experience reveals some of them to His children. The world cannot receive the Spirit of Truth by whom God reveals Himself; neither can the world know of His attributes which are revealed by measure to each one of His beloved children by His Spirit.

If we are manifested children of God, we have learned about some of His attributes. The precious scriptures bear witness with our witness which is within. Christ has all power in heaven and in earth, given to Him by His Father. He has power over all flesh, to give eternal life to as many as the Father gave unto Him before the world began. God is love, and He gives this love to His children. To say that God loves everybody is a lie. He hates Satan and his imps with a perfect hatred. He chose and rejected. He worked and none could stay His hand. His work is perfect. God willed to show forth His power and make His wrath known. He ordained every vessel of wrath that He might make known the riches of His grace on the vessels of mercy, which He had afore prepared unto glory. Why is this so? It seemed good in His sight and He gets pleasure out of His creation.

God gives the saints to believe on Him through the workings of His mighty power. He has created all things for Himself— without Him was not anything made that was made. He is here and there, even where the morning stars sing together. He is omnipresent—everywhere present. He is able to do exceeding abundantly above all that we ask or think through His power that worketh in us. God is beloved and worthy to receive glory and honor and praise from His children. He is a wonderful God, and a Father of His children. He has made His beloved Son to be unto His children wisdom, righteousness, sanctification and redemption. Christ is the Shepherd and Bishop of our soul, the Author and Finisher of our faith and salvation; yea, our all in all. Holy, just, and perfect in all His ways is our God. His Son is the truth, the resurrection, our life and our way if so be that the Spirit of God dwell in us—if so be He has given us to drink of the river of the water of Life freely, to taste the Good Word of God and power of the world to come.

He said that His thoughts are higher than our thoughts and His ways higher than our ways as the heavens are above the earth. God made two great lights, the greater light to shine by day and the lesser light to shine by night. He also made the stars. How infinite is our God! How incomprehensible is the Lord of this universe by feeble sense alone. Oh! The depth of the riches both of the wisdom and knowledge of our God. How unsearchable are His judgments and His ways past finding out.

Above all else, the divine attribute of God which makes this sinner cry out in hope is that He is a God of mercy. Mercy, yea, Divine Mercies of God. How wonderful that He is a God of Mercy. Maybe, just maybe, my case is not hopeless. Oh God, I hope you will be merciful to my unrighteousness and my sins and inequities you have remembered against me no more is my cry.

Is it just possible that we will awake in His likeness and be satisfied? Will He bless us to praise Him with a perfect praise in that bright land that shall never end? Will He bless us to love His Son to the very depths of our soul; to see Him as He is, and to behold His eternal glory when He comes again to receive the chosen few unto Himself that where He is there may they be also? I do not know the answer to these questions, but whether they be yes or no, God is God and perfect in all His ways.

The Doctrine of Absolute Predestination needs no defending. The dead can't hear it, and the living hear and believe it, because they are blessed of God with a hearing ear, a seeing eye, and an understanding heart. We can only hope that God will bless us to declare it to His children. This doctrine that is so strange to the natural man is a joy to those who believe in the finished work of Jesus Christ who bore witness to the truth, a truth that is as eternal, perfect, and unchangeable as our God. I am not afraid to declare that God predestinated the entrance of sin into the world just because sin exists. If God had not had a holy and divine purpose in sin, He would have left out the devil, vanity, temptation, and the weakness which is our in the flesh. But it pleased Him to create His children weak in the flesh, and that they might receive strength and all things, through their precious Saviour, the Lamb of God, to whom be glory both now and forever.

Did God create sin? Certainly. To deny His creation is to call God a liar because He alone is the Creator. Some say, "God is the creator of the wicked, but not of their wickedness." In other words, God created the wicked to do wickedly but they don't have to if they don't want to because they are free moral agents? I don't believe that. The wicked SHALL do wickedly, and none of the wicked shall understand about the things that be of God. If they had known who He was, they would not have taken and with wicked hands have crucified the Lord of glory, but only the wise understand. He created the wicked for the day of evil. To say otherwise is to deny the truth. He created the crooked serpent to tempt, and in my case I would yield to every temptation except for the grace of God.

God has a Holy purpose in our darkness as well as our light, our blindness as well as our sight, our weakness in the flesh as well as our strength in Christ, our hunger and thirst as well as our spiritual food and drink that comes alone from the Master's table. He is the ultimate source of all things, even the source of our strength to resist temptation. Without the manifestation of the new birth, we are nothing but sin, evil, and iniquity multiplied. We not only need to be forgiven for our sins, we need Him to give us a new heart and a new mind to go along with a glorified body before we will be prepared to go HOME to dwell in the house of the Lord forever. We need a loving heart, a Spiritual mind and body that we may rise to meet the Lord in the air when He comes for His friends and brethren on that glorious resurrection morning.

Lynwood Jacobs, June 2003

Re-edited, October 2009

ABSOLUTE PREDESTINATION—THE FOUNDATION OF GOD'S DOCTRINE

Just as love is the foundation upon which God built His church, I believe absolute predestination is the foundation upon which He built His doctrine. Remove the foundation of the omnipotent power and absolute will of God in all events in time and eternity and the rest of the doctrine will crumble into a confused rubble. All things then become a mish-mash of happenstance, rather that an orderly occurrence of events ordered in all things and sure by the perfect will of a perfect Workman. "...He is the rock, His work is perfect." Without absolute predestination, eternal life is an empty hope, election becomes man's choice, grace is a sometimes thing, and the principles of the doctrine of Christ are nothing more than fuel for debates.

God is omnipotent, which means He is unlimited in power and authority. "...for the Lord God omnipotent reignth." (Rev. 19:8) His reign is unlimited in heaven and earth and is not subject to the will, desire, or understanding of any creature in heaven or in earth. "...and He doeth according to His will among the inhabitants of the earth: and none can stay His hand, or say unto Him, what doest thou?" (Dan. 4:35)

God is absolute. He is free from limit, restriction, and qualification. He either predestinated all things or nothing. His sovereignty is absolute or non-existent. Being absolute, He did not will some events in time and eternity and not will all events. (Some say He chooses to wait around to find out what is going to happen next. How foolish)

To me, the greatest leaven ever placed in the doctrine of absolute predestination is found in the London Confession of Faith. This Confession of Faith is one of the most remarkable collections of truth and error that has ever been compiled in the name of religion. Though fact outweighs fiction, and profound understanding tends to hide the myths and notions therein, yet its true beauty shines out of darkness, and its clarity is marred by confusion. God alone knows why such a potentially great work contains so much leaven. It has some of the most beautiful and profound statements outside the Bible so that many of the writers must have been inspired by the Holy Spirit. It also contains some equally profound contradictions so that Satan must have been at the writer's table also. Many of our churches and associations took their articles of faith directly or indirectly from the London Confession of Faith. I believe that in a few cases some tares were pulled with the wheat.

The Confession states that God decreed all things, then states that He did not decree anything.

Truth: "God hath decreed in Himself from all eternity, by the most wise and holy counsel of His own will, freely and unchangeable, all things whatsoever come to pass." Art. I, Chapter 3 (in part).

Error: "Although God knoweth whatsoever may or can come to pass upon all supposed conditions, yet hath He not decreed anything, because He foresaw it as future, or as that which would come to pass upon such conditions." Art. 2, Chapter 3. (It is one eternal now with God)

In the above two statements, I believe the writers of the truth worshipped an absolute God, and the writers of the error worshipped a limited God. Hopefully, I worship the one only living and true God who is absolute. No limited god can reach my case, so I have no desire to worship such, or be identified with those who do. Their god is not my

God. Even so, I hope and deeply desire that this is spoken in love from a broken and contrite heart.

The writers listed many of the divine attributes of God stating emphatically that He is most absolute and works all things according to His own immutable will and council. Then they attempted to limit and restrict His immutable council and will.

Truth: "The Lord our God is…most absolute, working all things according to the council of His own immutable and most righteous will…" Art. 1, Chapter 2 (in part).

Error: "…yet, so as thereby is God neither the author of sin, nor hath fellowship with any therein; nor is violence offered to the will of the creature, nor yet is the liberty or contingency of second causes taken away, but rather established, in which appears His wisdom in disposing all things, and power and faithfulness in accomplishing His decree." Art. 1, Chapter 3 (in part).

Of all the leaven in the London Confession of Faith, probably none exceeds that contained in this last statement. Men have gone to great lengths to defend the statement: "…yet so as thereby is God neither the author of sin…" I once heard a man say that he had worried about the statement until he was given this thought: "God is not the author of sin, because He is under no law, so He cannot sin." Such a thought is so superfluous as to be little short of being foolish. Who in the true church has ever accused God of sinning? I can't find where even Satan has accused God of sinning. Some called Christ a sinner, but not God the Father. Why then is a statement required that says God is not a sinner, if indeed that is what the words mean.

The word **author** can mean creator which is the only way the word can be reasonably applied to God the Creator. "For by Him were ALL Things created, that are in heaven, and that are in earth, visible and invisible, whether they be thrones, or principalities, or powers; ALL things were created by Him, and for Him." (Col. 1:16)

To create means to bring into existence or being. For sin to come into existence, a weak, vain, and lustful human being subject to a law and a liar had to be created. For sin to continue, it requires the same things. God created every human being weak, vain, and lustful in nature. I find it impossible to believe that He would expect such a creature to be Spiritually strong and free from covetousness. God gave the law, and He formed the liar. Did He do so blindly, wondering at the results, and "hoping" that His purpose would ripen fast? How foolish the thought! The truth is that every weak, vain, and lustful human being is the perfect creation of a perfect God—for the purpose that they were created.

I am a sinner and need to be forgiven for my sins, one who is ten thousand talents in debt without a farthing to pay. My need to be forgiven for my sins is not the end of my need for Christ. Rather it is the beginning of my total need for Him.

Sin is the outward manifestation of my inward weakness. I not only need forgiveness for sins, I need inward strength. My need for Christ is not based on sin alone, if I am a child of God. He has forgiven the sins of His people. "For I will be merciful to their unrighteousness, and their sins and their iniquities will I remember no more." (Heb. 8:12) My need for Christ is because of my stony heart.

Sin is the stench that flows from my corrupted being. I not only need forgiveness for sin, I need incorruption. My need for Christ is because of my corruptible being.

Sin measures my inability to resist Satan's temptations. I need to be delivered from the power of Satan into the glorious liberty of the children of God.

Sin shows the midnight darkness of my blind soul. I need light to shine out of that darkness and eyes to see that light in others.

I need Christ to change my soul, spirit, and body, to put off the old man and put on the new. I need strength, incorruption and wisdom from above. I need Him to shod my feet with preparation of the gospel of peace, to gird my loins about with truth, to give me a breastplate of righteousness, and a helmet of salvation. I need Him to be my way, my stay and staff, my husband, friend, and brother.

Above all, I need Him to be the Lord my Righteousness, my all in all, that I might love and be loved as He loved. "Forgive me, Oh Lord! Then deliver me from the body of this death. Save me or I perish!" is my cry.

I have at this moment no desire to either deny my very being nor ask of Him, "Why hast thou made me thus?" My hope is that He has given me a desire to understand a revealed measure of His works, not question them nor try to limit Him in anything. God is not now, nor has He ever been, nor will He ever be a begging, pleading, restricted, limited, or conditional God. All events in time and eternity are the orderly disposal of the will and desire of a perfect Creator. May He bless me to rest my case on this foundation.

There is but one cause—Almighty God. The rest are results.

Because God formed man weak in the flesh, the result is that man is weak in the flesh. Because God gives His people inward strength through Jesus Christ, the result is their strength through Him.

Because God made man subject to vanity, the result is that the natural man has a soul that is empty and without Spiritual fruit. Because God frees His people from vanity by the gift of the Holy Spirit, the result is that they that have the Spirit do manifest the fruits of the Spirit.

Because God formed man mortal and corruptible, the result is that man is mortal and corruptible. Because God gave His people the victory through Jesus Christ, the result is that they shall put on immortality and incorruption.

Because God gave man a holy law that none could keep to a jot and tittle, the result is that all are lawbreakers. Because Christ kept and fulfilled the law to a jot and tittle, the result is that His brethren are not under the law, but under grace.

Because God formed Satan to lie and to tempt, the result is that Satan lies and tempts. Because God gave Christ the power to destroy Satan and his works, the result is that Christ destroyed the power of Satan over His people. I believed Satan's lies, not because I thought they were the truth, but because I knew nothing else. With the Apostle Paul, I did it ignorantly, and in unbelief. Now, if I am what I hope I am, that excuse has ended. If He keeps me by faith, no longer do I yield to every temptation. If His strength is mine, by measure of the gift of Christ, it is sufficient.

Because God made man subject to a carnal mind, the result is that all are carnal, sold under sin. Because God gives His people a Spiritual mind, the result is that they have life and peace and freedom from sin in Jesus Christ.

Because God created every human being to sin, the result is that all have sinned and come short of the glory of God. If God was not the creator of sin, who was? It shows me my total need for Jesus Christ, for which hopefully I am thankful.

I don't know what the writers of the London Confession of Faith meant when they stated that God has no fellowship for sinners. The truth is that those who are dead in sin have no fellowship with God. When quickened by Him, even when dead in sin, by faith, hope and charity we find peace with God and the end everlasting life.

"God's wisdom in disposing all things, and power and faithfulness in accomplishing His decrees." Does not appear in second causes, but appears in the MANIFESTED decrees, promises, and gifts of a covenant keeping triune Godhead. There is no such thing as second causes or other causes, which are nothing more than the results of God's Holy purpose which He purposed in His righteous will and Self before the world was.

The Spirit exercises the child of God. The child of God does not exercise the Spirit.

"The doctrine of this high mystery of predestination is to be handled with special prudence and care that men, attending the will of God revealed in His work, and yielding obedience thereunto, may from the certainty of their effectual vocation be assured of their eternal election: so shall this doctrine afford matter of praise, reverence and admiration of God, and of humility, diligence and abundant consolation to all that sincerely obey the gospel." Art. 7, Chapter 3.

This whole article is so foreign to my understanding, and contrary to my belief that I fear to even try to comment on it. Hopefully God will give me the great measure of charity I need to do so.

My only comment on the word **handled** is that the power of God "handles" the doctrine, not man.

Mankind does not **attend** the will of God, but **does** the will of God. His people do the will of God revealed in their heart and experience, and attested to by the Bible, not vice versa.

There is no certainty in anything in this life with reference to my effectual vocation. The only certainty is that what God doeth, it shall be forever. Nothing can be put to it, nor anything taken from it.

I have no assurance of eternal election, but I hope to have a hope in an eternally electing God. I cannot volunteer humility. If so, it would be a voluntary humility that every child of God could see through and know it for what it was—the fruits of the flesh. If I am humble, it is because God has abased me. I have exalted myself as high as the eagle and made my nest among the stars, but He has abased me, I hope.

Doctrine does not afford praise, admiration, and reverence of God. They that worship God in Spirit and in Truth praise, honor, and glorify Him.

God's people do not obey the gospel; they obey love in Christ. The new commandment is with power. It does not beg for obedience, but the will of God demands obedience and the power of God grants both the faith and the obedience of faith to His people.

The Lord Jesus Christ Himself and God even the Father has given everlasting consolation and good hope through grace unto His people. This is a living hope in a living God given to a living people who are alive unto God through Jesus Christ. May I be counted in that number!

The doctrine of absolute predestination was given by God to His Church for understanding. The unregenerated who use it only as a stump to hide their foolishness do so to the just condemnation to which they were ordained.

"Teach me, O Lord, the way of Thy statutes; and I shall keep it to the end. Give me understanding, and I shall keep Thy law: yea, I shall observe it with my whole heart. Make me to go in the path of Thy commandments; for therein do I delight. Incline my heart unto Thy testimonies, and not to covetousness. Turn away mine eyes from beholding vanity; and quicken thou me in the say." (Psa. 119:33-37)

Lynwood Jacobs

Editorial in Zion's Landmark-1974

JEWS

This proposal has been made: "All Jews are going to heaven, and all Gentiles that accept Christ as their personal saviour will go with them." The first part of the proposition may be partially true, depending on one's definition of a Jew. The Apostle Paul defined a Jew as follows: "For he is not a Jew, which is one outwardly; neither is that circumcision, which is outward in the flesh: But he is a Jew, which is one inwardly; and circumcision is that of the heart, in the Spirit, and not in the letter, whose praise is not of men, but of God." (Romans 2:28, 29). All who meet this definition of a Jew are children of God and heaven is their eternal home. As far as those who are Jews because of a lineage to Abraham, only a remnant will be saved according to the election of grace. (Rom.9:11&11:5) "For in Christ Jesus neither circumcision availeth anything, nor uncircumcision, but a new creature." (Gal .6:15, also see Col. 3:11.) To imply that one is going to heaven because of circumcision or natural lineage is wrong and not true according to a new creature called Apostle Paul. He had been Saul, a practicing Jew of the first order according to the letter until one day on the road near to Damascus; he was bathed in a heavenly Light and soon was made a Jew inwardly.

As far as the second part of the proposition, let us use the Apostle Paul as an example of how wrong it is to say that one must accept Christ as his personal saviour in order to be saved. As Saul he hated Christians with a perfect hatred and took part in an effort to destroy them from the earth. (See Acts 9:1, 2.) Suddenly, Christ appeared unto him and turned his world upside down. Then Saul was told by Christ to go into Damascus where, "it shall be told thee what thou MUST do." After 3 days without sight, food, or water, Saul was approached by a prepared Ananais who said, "Brother Saul, the Lord, even Jesus, that appeared unto thee in the way as thou camest, hath sent me that thou mightest receive thy sight, and be filled with the Holy Ghost." The scales fell from Saul's eyes and he received sight, and was baptized. (It is evident that he was baptized with Christ's baptism because he was filled with the Holy Ghost) In a few days he began to preach Christ in the synagogues, "that He is the son of God." Soon Saul was named Paul, an Apostle whose messages have brought great joy through the ages to his Gentile brethren, and one who endured much tribulation in his journey on earth to serve them.

Did Saul accept Christ as his personal saviour? No. Was he made accepted in the beloved? Yes. Christ was ordained his saviour before the world began. Paul's letter to the Saints at Ephesus is one of many total disclaimers to the notion that one must accept Christ as his personal saviour in order to be saved. This one statement from the book of Ephesians destroys free-willism to a believer: "According as He has chosen US in Him before the foundation of the world, that we should be holy and without blame before Him in love." (Eph.1:4) Is the US mentioned here those that will accept Christ as some might maintain? No. The US mentioned here are the Saints at Ephesus, the faithful in Christ Jesus and their kindred in Christ in all ages of time. God made the choice of His Saints, and not man.

A local preacher used as his text Ephesians 1 and caused uproar among his large congregation. We were told that a big tithing acquaintance who was a member of the church asked, "If salvation is free, why am I wasting all this money?" We said nothing, but it was a good question, especially since God is not worshiped in temples made with hands, neither is He worshiped with men's hands as though He needed anything.

Lynwood Jacobs

February 2010

JAMES

The book of James is one of the most unusual books in the Bible to me. Some Primitive Baptists in our area seem to use it almost exclusively. They justify it by saying "Well, it's in the Bible." The trouble is that some of James' writing to the twelve tribes of Israel is in contrast to what Paul wrote to the Gentiles. Unless I have misinterpreted James' writings, it seems to me he is not only giving some good advice, but also is often urging one to exercise the Spirit, which is impossible. The Holy Spirit exercises the born- again child of God, and is the only force that saves souls eternally.

In the last two verses of the Book of James (James 5:19, 20) he wrote, "Brethren, if any of you do err from the truth, and one convert him; Let him know, that he which converteth the sinner from the error of his way shall save a soul from death, and shall hide a multitude of sins." Nowhere does James indicate the need for the Holy Spirit from God to save a soul from death. To err from the truth is to lie. Christ alone hid the multitude of sins of His brethren when He died on the cross. Paul believed that it is impossible for those who were once enlightened and have tasted of the heavenly gift, to renew them unto repentance if they should fall away! God's gift of eternal life is to His children. They cannot "backslide" to destruction, because they are kept by the everlasting power and Spirit of God which is in them.

Paul wrote, "That the God of our Lord Jesus Christ, the Father of glory, may give unto you the spirit of wisdom and revelation in the knowledge of Him: the eyes of your understanding being enlightened; that ye may know what is the hope of His calling, and what is the riches of the glory of His inheritance in the saints, and what is the exceeding greatness of His power to us-ward who believe according to the workings of His mighty power." (Eph. 1:17-19) A child of God has his soul saved when GOD puts His love in his mind and heart through the gift of the Holy Ghost. The love of God is the most powerful spiritual force in the world, and it blesses one to bring forth Spiritual fruit unto God and the end everlasting life. Christ's death on the cross put the sins of His brethren as far away as the east is from the west, because He had covenanted with His Father to do so before the world was. The Comforter, which is the Holy Ghost, reveals the things of God and Christ to God's children, and not some self-appointed "Christ" going around saving souls for a price. To deny the power of the Holy Ghost in regeneration is blasphemy.

"Submit yourselves therefore to God. Resist the devil and he will flee from you. Draw nigh unto God, and He will draw nigh to you. Cleanse your hands, ye sinners; and purify your hearts, ye double minded." (James 4:7, 8)

Eliphaz the Temanite, a miserable comforter, told Job basically the same things that James is telling us above. An example, "Acquaint now thyself with Him, and be at peace: thereby good shall come unto thee." Job answered him with these words: "Behold, I go forward, but He is not there; and backward, but I cannot perceive Him: On the left hand, where He doth work, but I cannot behold Him, He hideth Himself on the right hand, that I cannot see Him: But He knoweth the way that I take: when He hath tried me I shall come forth as gold." (Job 23:8-10) Job confessed that he tried to submit himself to God to plead his case, but could not find Him. Neither can we find Him. The apostle Paul confirmed this when he said when he would do good, evil was present with him, and how to perform that which was good he found not. We are God's creation and He has appointed all the ways we must endure, even our afflictions. Job was learning that the trial of his faith was more precious than gold, and that Christ gives that peace that passes all understanding.

If James was here, I would ask him, "What does a sinner use to cleanse his hands? How does a sinner purify his heart? How does a sinner resist the devil when he enjoys his offerings so much?" Some would say a sinner can cleanse his hands and purify his heart by accepting Christ as his personal saviour. This is erring from the truth, called lying. The natural man receiveth not the things of the Spirit of God; neither can he know them, for they are spiritually discerned, and foolishness to him. The new birth is necessary for the elect to be made acceptable unto God through Christ Jesus, not the other way around. His children become a manifested saint because of what God ordained for Christ and the Holy Spirit to do for them, and not for what they can do for Him.

Lynwood Jacobs

March 2011

JAMES 1:13-15, ETC.

"Let no man say when he is tempted, I am tempted of God: for God cannot be tempted with evil, neither tempteth He any man: But every man is tempted, when he is drawn away of his own lust and enticed. Then when lust hath conceived, it bringeth forth sin, and sin, when it is finished, bringeth forth death.

God is truth. The truth does not tempt to evil. It takes a lie to tempt. God cannot lie. He can and did create a liar called a serpent, or Satan, or the devil, or an evil spirit, etc. (Job 26:13-14) That evil spirit lied to Eve in the Garden of Eden and has been lying and tempting mankind ever since. (See I Kings 22:22-23.) Adam and Eve yielded to temptation because they were yet in the flesh and subject to vanity. They were of the earth, earthy. If they had been born again of God at this point, their desire would have been for the fruit of the Tree of Life because they had permission from God to eat of it, and would have lived forever. (See Gen. 2:9, 16.) Had they done so, there would have been no need for Christ to come and pay that terrible penalty for their sins which was laid on Him before the world began. (Eph. 1:4 & Heb. 9:14) Christ did not say that all but Adam and Eve must be born again. He said the new birth is a must for anyone to become a manifested, loving child of God and that included our two common ancestors. (See I John 4:7.)

James wrote that faith without works is dead. The Apostle Paul taught that works without faith are dead. I happen to prefer Paul's version, though both are truth. I'm the same way about that called the Lord's Prayer. I prefer the version that ends in: For Thine is the Kingdom, and the power and the glory forever. (Math. 6:13) The other version does not end with those words, but both versions are the truth.

James said be ye doers of the word and not hearers only, deceiving your own selves. I'm like Paul, when I would do good, evil is present with me, and how to perform that which is good I find not. On the morning of the resurrection, those who sue for entrance based on their dead works are going to be told, "I never knew you: depart from me, ye that work iniquity." (See Math. 7:21-23.) The same act can be a godly deed or a dead work depending on its driving force. If the love of God is the driving force, the deed is good and the doer does not need a pat on the back or a rosy feeling.

James said resist the devil, and he will flee from you. I believe I have been blessed by grace to resist the devil at times, but he keeps throwing temptations at me daily. I will yield to temptation unless kept by the power of a God-given faith unto salvation ready to be revealed in the last day.

James' letter was addressed to the twelve tribes which were scattered abroad. The other Apostles' letters were to the saints, to the faithful in Christ Jesus, to the beloved of God, to them who are sanctified in Christ, called to be saints, to the various churches, to the strangers scattered about, to the elect, to the general assembly and church of the first born, and to the blessed of God. I'm not a member of one of the twelve tribes, but I have a hope that I am a member of the family of God for whom the New Testament was written, who are free indeed. That is why I prefer the writings of the other Apostles to James who wrote a few things that I don't believe are possible. (See James 4:7-9.) He was also blessed to send some profound thoughts and good advice to the twelve tribes who were not free but still under the Law.

Lynwood Jacobs

December 2006

TRANSGRESSION

In Rom. 14:23 there is hidden one of the most profound statements found in the writings of the Apostle Paul. "...for whatsoever is not of faith is sin." They that are in the flesh cannot please God, because they do not have faith. But they are not in the flesh, but in the Spirit if so be that the Spirit of God dwell in them. Faith is a gift of God! It is the Holy Spirit of God that reveals the things of God to His children. It is Christ in them that gives them a hope of that life and immortality which He brought to light through the gospel of peace. Until the love of God is shed abroad in our heart by the Holy Ghost, which is given us of God, we cannot keep the commandment of love. A law is a rule of action. The law of the Spirit of life in Christ Jesus rules the action of a child who is born of God, for it is the same law of love that ruled His actions. A manifested child of God loves God, loves Christ, and loves their brethren.

Sin is the transgression of the law. The laws written on tables of stone were given by God that sin might abound. What does it do? It condemns us who transgress, and exalts Christ, who not only did not transgress but fulfilled the law and the prophets to a jot and a tittle! To a child of God it makes the electing grace of God abound by revealing unto them their total need for the saving grace which is alone in Christ Jesus. It makes God's children know that they can only keep the first two, the commandments of love, if they have been born of God, not of corruptible seed, as is their first birth in the flesh. If God has written His law in our heart and imprinted it in our mind, we have by measure of God the law of love to rule our actions, and give us a living faith in a living God and

His Son who have loved the chosen remnant with everlasting love.

Apply "for whatsoever is not of faith is sin" to Adam and Eve and it will draw you closer to them. Their need for Christ, for God's love from the new birth, and for His mercy, grace and compassion was one with our need for the same things.

Lynwood Jacobs

April 2009

ACTS 3:20, 21

Acts 3:20, 21: And He shall send Jesus Christ, which before was preached unto you: Whom the heaven must receive until the times of restitution of all things, which God hath spoken by the mouth of all His holy prophets since the world began.

The words of these two verses of scripture tell plainly that Jesus Christ is alive, He is in heaven, He will return at the appointed time of God, and that He was preached on in the world. Restitution of all things is not as plainly understood.

The word **restitution** has two basic meanings as follows:

1. Restoring anything to its rightful owner. Example: The Jews claim they are the rightful owners of the "Holy Land" as described in the Old Testament. They want it restored to them. The Arabs claim they were there before the Jews and want to keep the land. In any case, this is just one thing and not the *all things* spoken of in Acts 3:21.

2. Replacing a lost or damaged item with something of equal value. Example: I killed your cow and had nothing of equal value to replace her. My friend offered to pay you $100 for the dead cow, and you were satisfied. In like manner, I was 10,000 talents in debt without a farthing to pay. A Friend paid the 10,000 talents with something of greater value and now my debt is forgiven. I felt forever indebted to only my Friend, until He showed "your redemption came by Me but was from above." Where my sins abounded, God's grace did much more abound. Christ's sacrifice paid my debt, I hope, and the debt

of every child of God, even those who are not yet born into this world.

All things work together for good to God's children who are being prepared for immortality and the world to come. The following are a few of the multitude of "things" ordained of God for the perfecting of the Saints:

They were deaf, until they were given a hearing ear.

They were blind until they received a seeing eye.

They were lost until they were made to worship God in Spirit and in Truth.

They loved mortality until they were dressed in immortality.

They did not understand corruption until they knew incorruption.

They were satisfied with the image of Adam until they were given a desire to be in the image of Christ

They thought they loved until they were given true Love.

They worshipped gods until they were blessed to worship God.

They trusted in their own power until they tasted of the good word of God and the power of the world to come.

They thought man willed and God wished and wanted until God showed them that He willed and they wish and want.

They thought they understood until the operation came that replaced their stony heart with a heart of understanding.

They thought God's sovereignty covered some things until they learned that it covers all things in heaven and on earth.

They thought you had to choose Christ until they were made to hope that He chose them.

God's Kingdom will be restored when it is fully manifest and prepared of God for the return of Christ. Then He will come again to carry the Family of God HOME to dwell in the House of the Lord forever, and so shall we ever be with the Lord. What a glorious hope that through the grace of Almighty God we will be in that elect number!

Lynwood Jacobs

January 2004

EXPERIENCE

On July 30, 1960, a quiet inner voice told me to quit my 7-year job as a successful Allstate insurance agent. I had just been elected Commander of a 1500 member American Legion Post. I walked away into an unknown future, strangely submissive to the force that was to change my life forever.

In April, 1963, I was at home pealing pine posts with a drawing knife, preparing them to stack, dry and treat. I glanced over the field to the west and saw 4 banners go by in the air. The first had Granddad, the second had Aunt Zula, the third had Mama, and the fourth had Daddy inscribed on it. Puzzled, I went back to pealing posts. Soon those same 4 banners went by in the air again. Now the first one had Brother Pete, the second had Sister Zula, the third had Sister Gladys, and the fourth had Brother Curtis inscribed on it. As I turned away, I was told to go down on my knees and ask God for forgiveness. Aloud I said "No." Immediately a sack-like membrane formed in my stomach and filled up and started up my throat. It stopped and choked me to my knees and I could not breathe. I was made to cry out Lord forgive me of my sins or I die. What was choking me to my knees then moved on up and out and I could breathe again. I was then overcome with a glorious rapture I had never known before. The short distance to my granddad's house was covered without touching the ground, or so it felt. Through tears, I related my experience to Brother Pete and Sister Zula, my grandfather and great aunt. Later, I related it to Sister Gladys and Brother Curtis, my mother and father.

The next meeting day I related my experience to the brethren at Mount Pisgah Primitive Baptist church with no intention of asking for a home with them. That "no intention" was overruled, and my 87-year-old grandfather, Elder Peter Hiram Jacobs, baptized me the 3rd Sunday in April, 1963. My world was now completely turned upside down. I had come to love those old fogies I once seldom visited, and found no greater joy in the world than to be with them.

In October of 1966, liberated but not ordained, I left school on Friday where I taught and headed toward Tomball, TX, to the Union Association. As I drove west toward Beaumont on I-10, I began to see a child being clothed with the whole armor of God. The rapture was so great that I missed my turn on US 90 and drove another 40 or more miles toward Houston. When I realized where I was, I was forced to find a new way to the church. With all that, I felt sure that when I got to the church I would be the first one called on, and man, did I have something to tell the congregation. Sure enough, I was the first one called upon, but it did not turn out as I had expected. No sooner than the word armor came out of my mouth, an old fashion curtain came down before my eyes, and I could not even call Elder Paul Weisinger's name to tell him to get somebody in the stand that could preach. That experience taught me two great lessons. One, Lynwood can't preach. Two, God gives us experiences along the way that are just for us. A secondary lesson was that God's will is the best driver anywhere, even on busy I-10.

One Sunday in 1966 Granddad said, "I want brother Lynwood to open services." I thought he had lost his mind. Protesting all the way, I was escorted to the stand. As I stood there these words came out of my mouth: "We have received, not the spirit of the world, but the Spirit which is of God, that we might know the things that are freely given us of God, which things also we speak, not in words which man's wisdom teacheth, but which the Holy Ghost teacheth, comparing spiritual things with spiritual." After a few comments I sat down convinced that was the end of that. I barely noticed that there was hardly a dry eye in the house. A month later I was called on again. My aggravation disappeared when the cross appeared before my eyes and Christ was on it. He looked at me and spoke these words, "My Father so loved you that He gave Me that you might have everlasting life." Then He died as I looked upon His precious body with the crown of thorns on His head. At that moment I did not fully realize that I had been telling what I was seeing. Overcome with emotion, I knew then that I could never again deny any call to the stand. On the 3rd Sunday in January, 1967 I was ordained an Elder in the Primitive Baptist Church.

In June 1967 the Jacobs reunion was to be held at Fields at our house on 2nd Saturday. My plans were to leave the reunion after lunch and go to Huntington to their 3 day meeting. At 6 AM that morning as I was walking next door to drink coffee, I was told to get my clothes and go to Huntington, doubting nothing. I told Bennie and Mama what had happened, and went to Huntington. At time for services, I looked around, and I was the only elder there, and I had been ordained less than 6 months. Elder D.B. Wallace, their Moderator had cracked his ribs when he fell on the way down on Friday. Elder Paul Weisinger had the dates mixed up. Elder Cecil Jacobs had not planned to come because of the reunion. The fact is they had no preach service Friday, and I was the only elder there Saturday morning, afternoon, night, and Sunday morning and communion service. I learned from that experience to never doubt an unction concerning the church.

Lynwood Jacobs

2009

FAVORITES

May this writing give you to recall and meditate on some of your favorite scriptures. To me this is almost equal to being with my brethren. Here are some of my favorites.

"The grace of the Lord Jesus Christ, and the love of God, and the communion of the Holy Ghost be with you all. Amen." (2 Cor. 13:14) If I could choose any words to bid my brethren goodbye from this world it would be these from the Apostle Paul. Grace, love, and spiritual communion with those you have been given to love. What a great joy just to think on these things!

"But the God of all grace, who hath called us unto His eternal glory by Christ Jesus, after that ye have suffered a while, make you perfect, stablish, strengthen, settle you. (1 Peter 5:10) The God of all grace calls with a holy calling, not according to our works, but according to His own purpose in grace which was given us in Christ Jesus before the world began. (See 2 Tim. 1:9.) (Another favorite scripture). Christ said that in this world we would have tribulations, but for His Brethren not to fear because He had overcome the world. They overcome the world when given to believe in Him, when they are stablished in the faith. They are strengthened with might by His Spirit in the inner man, Christ in them the hope of glory. They will not be settlers in this world. God will settle them forever in that land that is very far off, where they shall see the King in His beauty and the Son will welcome them with open arms. Faith and hope will no longer be needed, and the perfecting and delivery of the Saints will be complete.

"Behold what manner of love the Father hath bestowed upon us, that we should be called the sons of God:

therefore the world knoweth us not, because it knew Him not. Beloved, now are we the sons of God, and it doth not appear what we shall be: but we know that, when He shall appear, we shall be like Him: for we shall see Him as He is." (1 John 3:1, 2) WE SHALL BE LIKE HIM. These beautiful words should be enough to stop the endless conjecture about what His brethren will be like in the resurrection. They will be like Him and be satisfied. WE SHALL SEE HIM AS HE IS. Oh, glorious last day when we shall see Him as He is, when our hope is fulfilled, and we behold the glorified Son of our Father who is alive forevermore.

"God that made the world and all things therein, seeing that He is Lord of heaven and earth, dwelleth not in temples made with hands; Neither is worshipped with men's hands, as though he needed anything, seeing He giveth to all life, and breath, and all things; And hath made of one blood all nations of men for to dwell on the face of the earth, and hath determined the times before appointed, and the bounds of their habitation." (Acts 17:24-26) According to these inspired words of the Apostle Paul this is God's world, and all things therein are His, even you and me. We are His and we are here for whatever purpose He has in us. I hope we are counted among those that He has formed for Himself, to show forth His praise. He is not worshipped with the fruits of the labor of the natural man, because He needs us for nothing, but we need Him for all things. To say that God wants, or wishes, or will-if-you-let-Him, is blasphemy of the worst order. Why? because it denies the power of the Holy Ghost in regeneration. It is impossible for a man to born himself again! Paul says that God has determined the times before appointed. This is the absolute predestination of God. To everything there is a season and a time to every purpose under the heavens, for all things are ordained of God, nothing left out. The simplicity in this statement is easy for even a new born child of God to understand.

"Father, I will that they also, whom thou hast given me, be with me where I am; that they may behold my glory, which thou hast given Me: for thou lovedst me before the foundation of the world." (John 17:24) "And the glory which thou gavest Me I have given them; that they may be one, even as We are one." (John 17:2) We must be glorified to ever behold His glory as the only begotten Son of God. When He gives us His Spirit, then we become one with Him and our precious brethren. This unity in love is what we seek among our brethren, that we may love one another as He loved us. God's love may sustain when we are alone, but it reaches its peak when we are blessed to share in the true unity of the Spirit that binds us to one another, to Christ, and through Him to God. This will sustain us until we are blessed to be where Christ is now, that we may be united with Him in His God given Glory throughout all ages, world without end. This is my hope.

Lynwood Jacobs

2011

EDITORIAL ZIONS'S LANDMARK, 1976

"All Thy works shall praise Thee, O Lord, and Thy saints shall bless Thee. They shall speak of the glory of Thy kingdom, and talk of Thy power, To make known to the sons of men His mighty acts, and the glorious majesty of His kingdom. Thy kingdom and Thy dominion endureth throughout all generations." (Psalm 145:10-13)

These beautiful words of the psalmist have inspired the hearts of saints in every generation. Faithful Abraham was not the only one to seek a city with foundation, whose builder and maker is God (See Heb. 11:10.) By the same God-given faith the psalmists and many in this day look for that kingdom where they hope to see the King in His beauty, and behold the land that is very far off. (See Isa. 33:17.)

This everlasting Kingdom of God in all its sanctified glory is the promise to every saint that has been given to praise God in spirit and in truth. "Fear not, little flock; for it is your Father's good pleasure to give you the kingdom." (Luke 12:32) "But the hour cometh, and now is when the true worshippers shall worship the Father in spirit and in truth..." (John 4:23)

The mighty acts of the Triune Godhead are administering an entrance into this glorious kingdom for every Saint. The Apostle Peter said, "For so an entrance shall be ministered unto you abundantly into the everlasting kingdom of our Lord and Saviour Jesus Christ." (II Peter 1:11)

As the sainted subjects are being fitted for that kingdom, they have their hopes laid only on the mighty works of God. The psalmist testified, "I will speak of the glorious honor of Thy majesty, and of Thy wondrous works." (Psalm 145:5) They ascribe salvation to God even as that innumerable host that the Apostle John beheld, "After this I beheld, and lo, a great multitude, which no man could number, of all nations, and kindreds, and people, and tongues, stood before the throne, and before the Lamb, clothed with white robes, and palms in their hands, and cried with a loud voice, saying Salvation to our God which sitteth upon the throne, and unto the Lamb." (Rev. 7:9, 10)

They say, "Amen" with those that declare, "…Blessing, and glory, and wisdom, and thanksgiving and honour, and power, and might, be unto our God forever. Amen." (Rev. 7:12)

When one of His disciples said unto Him, "Lord, teach us to pray." Christ answered him, thusly, "When ye pray, say, Our Father which art in heaven, Hallowed be Thy name. Thy kingdom come…" (Luke 11:12) As God's will unravels on the pages of time, His kingdom must come for those He has loved and drawn with an everlasting love," "Yea, I have loved thee with an everlasting love—therefore, with loving kindness have I drawn thee." (Jer. 31:3)

The angel Gabriel said unto Mary, "…And He shall reign over the house of Jacob forever; and of His kingdom there shall be no end." (Luke 1:33) Only in Christ, the Sanctifier, do His sanctified brethren possess this kingdom which is His inheritance to share with those who are all of one with Him. "For both He that sanctifieth, and they who are sanctified are all of one; for which cause He is not ashamed to call them brethren." (Heb. 2:11) "In whom also we have an inheritance, being predestinated according to the purpose of Him who worketh all things after the council of His own will." (Eph. 1:11)

The Apostle Peter laid out the hope of this heavenly inheritance for every saint begotten of and kept by the power of God. "Blessed be the God and Father of our Lord Jesus Christ, which according to His abundant mercy hath begotten us again unto a lively hope by the resurrection of Jesus Christ from the dead, to an inheritance incorruptible, and undefiled, and that fadeth not away, reserved in heaven for you who are kept by the power of God through faith unto salvation ready to be revealed in the last time." (I Peter 1:3-5) Prophecy declared some names of the Ruler of this enduring Kingdom. It says that though He was to be manifest upon the earth, yet His goings forth were from everlasting. "For unto us a child is born, unto us a Son is given: and the government shall be upon His shoulder: and His name shall be called Wonderful, Councilor, The mighty God, The everlasting Father, The Prince of Peace." (Isa. 9:6) "But thou Bethlehem Ephratah, though thou be little among the thousands of Judah, yet out of thee shall He come forth unto me that is to be ruler in Israel; whose goings forth have been from of old, from everlasting." (Mica 5:2)

As the King walked the face of this earth in a body prepared for Him by God, He said, "My kingdom is not of this world." (John 18:36) He said, also, "The Kingdom of God is within you." (Luke 17:21) This inward kingdom which is not of this world is in those who are not of the world, even as He is not of the world. "They are not of the world, even as I am not of the world" (John 17:16) This inward kingdom is a seal of promise of the world which is to come and is not beholden to death, for its King has, through death, destroyed him that had the power of death. (See Heb. 2:14, 15.)

This inward kingdom breaks in pieces and consumes all other kingdoms, and it shall stand forever. (See Dan. 1:4.) It is invisible, yet the light of the body is the eye; therefore when thine eye is single, the whole body also is full of light..." (Luke 11:34)

This inward kingdom cannot be seen in others nor light shine forth from it until one is born again. "Except a man be born again he cannot see the Kingdom of God." (John 3:3) This new birth makes the eye single with love, since the planting of God's seed of love in a sinner's heart is the new birth with power. So this inward kingdom is one of love. It is not meat and drink, but righteousness and peace and joy in the Holy Spirit. (See Rom. 14:17.)

In this time world the saints have this treasure (kingdom) in earthen vessels, but for the world to come they must put on that tabernacle not made with hands, eternal in the heavens. "For God, who commanded the light to shine out of darkness, hath shined in our hearts, to give the light of the knowledge of the glory of God in the face of Jesus Christ. But we have this treasure in earthen vessels, that the excellency of the power may be of God, and not of us." (II Cor. 4:6, 7) "For we know that if the earthly house of this our tabernacle were dissolved, we have a building of God, an house not made with hands, eternal in the heavens." (II Cor. 5:11)

On the morning of the resurrection when Christ shall have raised their vile bodies and fashioned them like unto His glorious body, the saints will be clothed upon with that house not made with hands, eternal in the heavens. (See Phil. 3:21.) Then shall the righteous shine forth in the Kingdom of their Father. (Matt. 13:43) With that inward kingdom now cloaked in a glorified tabernacle they shall live forever in that heavenly kingdom that shall never end, eternal in the heavens. When they have been there ten thousand year, bright shining as the sun, they've no less days to sing God's praise than when they've first begun. (See Lloyd's Hymn, 355.)

This ingathering will be then, even as it is now, the work of God. "Fear not, for I am with thee: I will bring thy seed from

132

the east, and gather thee from the west. I will say to the north, Give up; and the south, Keep not back: bring My sons from far, and My daughters from the ends of the earth; Even every one that is called by My name: for I have created Him for my glory, I have formed him: yea, I have made him." (Isa. 43:5, 7)

The Apostle Paul tells us that in this life the saints have borne the image of the earthy, but in the life to come they shall bear the image of the heavenly. "As we have borne the image of the earthy, we shall also bear the image of the heavenly. If in this life only we have hope in Christ, we are of all men most miserable." (I Cor. 15:49, 19)

What a wonderful hope it is to believe that a way has been administered for God's people into that eternal Kingdom. That way is Christ. He has promised to return again, and receive His people unto Himself, that where He is now, there may they be also. (See John 14:1-3.)

What a wonderful trust has been given to God's people. They trust in His works, His power, His salvation, His resurrection and His way. "Trust in the Lord with all thine hear; and lean not unto thine own understanding. In all thy ways acknowledge Him, and He shall direct thy paths." (Psalm 3:5, 66)

Sometimes the path may seem dim, and the journey painful, wearisome and hopeless. Yet even this is not to be compared to the glory that shall be revealed in those that love God. When they see Him as they are seen, know Him as they are known, only then will they be truly satisfied. "As for me, I will behold thy face in righteousness: I shall be satisfied when I awake with thy likeness." (Psalm 17:15)

This is written in the hope that the glorious words from the 145th Psalm used as an introduction will find a place in the hearts of this present generation, "One generation shall praise Thy works to another, and shall declare Thy mighty works." (Psalm 145:4)

All of God's works praise Him. The blessed saints do bless Him. They speak of the glory of His Kingdom and talk of His power. He has made known to them His mighty acts. They have received the earnest of the inheritance by promise of the glorious majesty of His Kingdom. They have the surety that His Kingdom and dominion endureth forever. Their hope is rested on the promise that prayer to God is answered, when it comes from a heart crying, "Thy Kingdom come."

Lynwood Jacobs

January 19, 1976

PRECIOUS MEMORIES (THE RESURRECTION)

Published in the <u>Zion's Landmark</u>

March, 1974

Dear Elder Mewborn,

In the words of the poet, "Precious memories how they linger, how they ever flood my soul…" The three-day meetings we were blessed to attend in 1973 ended with the one in California at Bakersfield. When we read their minutes, their circular letter written by Sister Nancy Clay, as well as the letters by Brothers Walter Wilson and Harry Vories in the January Landmark, our cup was refilled by precious memories of that meeting.

We went to the meeting because God has given us a love for Brother Walter and Elder Jefferson. We want to go again, God willing, because He has given us a love for all the brethren and sisters we met. Brother Jeff and Sister Grace are truly a father and mother in Israel to all who know them among Absoluters. Brother Walter was our beloved Jonathan—he could not have been more thoughtful or considerate to our every need during our visit.

The 49ers struck veins of pure gold in the hills of California, but we struck veins of pure love in the hearts of wonderful brethren. To us this love is more precious than all the gold of Ophar.

Brother Mewborn, I have read with much interest the writings on the resurrection in the Landmark. No principle of the doctrine of Christ is more precious to the church than the resurrection of the dead. It is so much the center of our hope in Christ that it is understandable how overzealous brethren might make a mutual understanding of what we shall be like in the resurrection a test of fellowship between themselves and others. However, if there is one thing that is clear to me from a search of the Bible, it is that we do not know what we shall be like in the resurrection.

The Apostle John confirms this, "Beloved, now are we the sons of God, and IT DOTH NOT APPEAR WHAT WE SHALL BE, but we know that when He shall appear we shall be like Him; for we shall see Him as He is." (I John 3:2) This is the same John who saw Him with his eyes, looked upon Him, and his hands handled the Word of Life. (See I John 1:1, 2.) He was with the eleven to whom the risen Christ appeared. (Luke 24:36-51) Yet, John said he did not know what we shall be like when He shall appear.

The Apostle Paul called it a mystery. "Behold I shew you a mystery; we shall not all sleep, but we shall all be changed." (I Cor. 15:51) The Apostle did not clear up the mystery but rather heightened it for me when he said, concerning the resurrection of the body: "It is sown in corruption; it is raised in incorruption: It is sown in dishonour; it is raised in glory: It is sown in weakness; it is raised in power: It is sown a natural body; it is raised a spiritual body." (I Cor. 15:42-44)

I believe the same IT that is sown is the IT that is raised an incorruptible, glorified, spiritual body with power to ascend on high to ever be with the Lord. But, Brother Mewborn, I can't comprehend such an immortal and incorruptible being. All I seem to comprehend is a weak, natural body filled with corruption and dishonour.

King David expressed my hope, "As for me, I will behold thy face in righteousness: I shall be satisfied when I awake, with thy likeness." (Psalm 17:15) Not until the morning of the resurrection shall the children of God, with King David, behold

His face and see those bodies fashioned like unto His glorious body, be in His likeness, and be satisfied.

To those brethren and sisters to whom God has given a revelation of that glorious dawn I would say, "This was for you—to strengthen your hope and faith in the precious promises of God. Never use such revelations as a test of fellowship, but rather rejoice in the wonders of the glorious God for a season. Even the brightest revelation in this life is no more than seeing though a glass darkly, when compared to the glory that shall be revealed in God's people in that day.

As for me, I do not know what body, soul, or spirit I shall come forth with, but this I do know: "I know that whatsoever God doeth, it shall be forever: nothing can be put to it, nor anything taken from it..." (Ecc. 3:14) I believe God has already determined who shall come forth, immortal, incorruptible, glorified, with life and power to praise Him with perfect praise in that bright Kingdom that shall never end.

"But God giveth it a body as it hath pleased Him, and to every seed his own body." (I Cor. 15:38) The body that his sons and daughters shall come forth with shall be a gift of God, just as the Spirit that shall be the life of that body is a gift of God. Both are best left to the perfection of His ways until the glorious appearing of our Saviour Jesus Christ, who is the brightness of God's glory and the express image of His person.

"Blessed and holy is he that hath part in the first resurrection: on such the second death hath no power..." (Rev. 20:6) I believe that Christ's resurrection was the first resurrection, and I believe that everyone who was chosen in Him before the foundation of the world had a part in His resurrection. "Now if we be dead with Christ, we believe that we shall also live with Him." (Romans 6:8) When this newness of life is manifested to one dead in trespasses and in sin, he is said to be born again,

137

not of corruptible, but of incorruptible seed, by the word of God, who liveth and abideth forevermore. THIS NEW BIRTH MAKES MANIFEST YOUR PART IN CHRIST'S RESURRECTION. You are not dead to sin, but alive unto God through Jesus Christ your Lord. You are free from the Law of Sin and Death, and are under grace. In a spiritual sense you have passed from death unto life in the likeness of His resurrection. But you have this treasure in a tabernacle of clay, which must be put off, that you might be clothed upon with that house not built with hands, eternal in the heavens. Then and only then shall you know that the second death has no power over you, and with all the saints of God you can cry out in triumphant victory, "O death, where is thy sting, O grave, where is thy victory," as you ascend on high to drink forever from the River of Love.

Brother Mewborn, may God bless us to see you at Mobile, Alabama, the second week end in April. Those are lovely brethren and sisters, and I believe you will be glad you made the trip. I hope that I am your brother in hope, and that your God is my God, and your people my people.

(Elder) Lynwood Jacobs

February 18, 1974

DEFINITION OF HARDSHELL—Editorial

ZION'S LANDMARK

April, 1976

What is a Hardshell Baptist? The term "hardshell" has been applied for many years to the God-fearing people that I have been blessed to hope are my brethren (brothers and sisters) in Christ Jesus. It is used by some as a term of derision. Over the years my experience has made me believe that this term is correctly applied to those I call brethren in hope. I have heard many good thoughts about what the word "hardshell" means. I would like to express my beliefs and why I believe that the word aptly describes the child of God.

A shell is a covering that gives protection. If the shell is soft, the more apt it is to be pierced. If it does not full cover the one it protects, the wearer may be wounded or killed.

In I Samuel: 17 and Ephesians 6, I believe the difference between a softshell and a hardshell is made clear. A shell with chinks in it that affords little or no protection to the wearer, and a hardshell that affords total protection to the wearer is made plain.

As Goliath of Gad stood in a valley between the encamped armies of Israel on one mountain and the Philistines on a mountain on the other side, he fearlessly defied the armies of Israel saying, "…I defy the armies of Israel this day." (I Sam. 17:10) Goliath was a champion of the Philistines and he inspired dismay and fear in Israel. "When Saul and all Israel heard those words of the Philistine, they were dismayed and greatly afraid." (I Sam. 17:10)

What a fearful sight this nine-foot giant must have been clad in his mighty shell of armour which weighed nearly 150 pounds. What great fear that mighty spear with its twenty pound head must have brought to the heart of even the most valiant warrior in Israel's army. Who could stand against its terrible thrust or face the great sword at close hand? For forty days this fearsome sight bragged before the armies of Israel.

Then we hear the voice of a stripling of a lad, a shepherd of the flock, the youngest of Jesse's sons saying, "Is there not a cause? Let no man's heart fail because of him; thy servant will go and fight with this Philistine." (I Sam. 17:29 and 32) But where is David's armour? He refused the offer of Saul's armour. "I cannot go with these; for I have not proved them. And David put them off him." (I San, 17:39)

The mystery of David's shell of armour begins to clear as we see him standing before the Philistine and fearlessly declaring, "Thou comest to me with a sword, and with a spear, and with a shield: but I come to thee in the name of the Lord of hosts, the God of the armies of Israel, whom thou hast defied. This day will the Lord deliver thee into my hands—And all this assembly shall know that the Lord slayeth not with sword and spear: for the battle is the Lord's and He will give you into our hands."

Yes, David came into battle in a shell made up of the whole armour of God. His feet were shod with the preparation of the gospel of peace shown when he said, "...for the battle is the Lord's." His loins were girt about with the truth. "I come in the name of the Lord of hosts, the God of the armies of Israel." King David was to go forth many times during his life in the name of the Lord of hosts, and he always gave God credit for the victory. In the twilight of his life he was to say, "Thine, O Lord, is the greatness, and the power, and the victory, and the majesty.: for all that is in heaven and in the earth is Thine: Thine is the kingdom, O Lord, and Thou art exalted as head above all." (I Chron. 29:11) No wonder King David was a man after God's own heart.

David's breastplate was not of mail as was Goliath's, but it was the breastplate of righteousness, even the imputed righteousness of Almighty God that comes alone through the Lord Jesus Christ. Blessed is the man to whom the Lord will not impute sin." (Rom. 4:8) Nathan, the prophet, was to tell King David that his sins of adultery and murder were forgiven by God and that he would not die under the penalty of the law. "The Lord also hath put away thy sin; thou shalt not die." (II Sam. 12:13) God's eternal grace and mercy bathed David, the son of Jesse, as it did David, the King of all Israel.

As he stood before Goliath, David had on the helmet of salvation for he was the anointed of the Lord to take Saul's place when he died before the Philistine Army. Was there any doubt about the outcome, when David's sword was the sword of the Spirit of the Lord? (See Eph. 6:17.) This was the same sword of Zion and of Gideon that has ever stood against the enemy of God's elect and prevailed every time without fail.

David's shield was the shield of faith for he had said unto Saul, "The Lord that delivered me out of the paw of the lion, and out of the paw of the bear, He will deliver me out of the hand of this Philistine." (I Sam. 17:37)

Goliath's shell was the whole armour of man, and his trust was in the arm of flesh. David's shell was the armour of

God. His strength was of the Lord so the stone went straight and true to Goliath's weakness. As it sank into his forehead, Goliath's body fell to the earth with the seat of its wisdom destroyed. When the Philistines saw their champion was dead, they fled but to die. Is this not true today with men worshippers who trust in man and make flesh their arm? When their champions fall into death or corruption, they flee to another and another in a restless search for that which cannot be sought out and found by man's wisdom. Their shell is as Goliath of Gad, and it will not protect them in the day of temptation.

Every manifested child of God has a shell so hard that it protects forever. Their feet are shod with the preparation of the gospel of peace, and their loins are girt about with the Truth. They have on the breastplate of Righteousness and the helmet of Salvation. In their hand is the sword of the Spirit with which they are enabled to withstand in the evil day, and having done all, to stand. (See Eph. 6:13.)

I believe that every Hardshell Baptist not only wears the whole armour of God, but they have been baptized with the Holy Ghost and with fire. As such, they have received the victory in Christ Jesus. "But thanks be to God, which giveth us the victory through our Lord Jesus Christ." (I Cor. 15:57) Young David in his day, and we in our day, must receive the victory over death as a gift of God. If not, we are as Goliath of Gad. No matter how long or loud our boast, no matter how great our armour of self-righteousness, sooner or later a young Man slays us with the Truth right between the eyes.

If, however, our shell is the armour of God that David wore, it has been proven in the battle that is the Lord's, and the victory that is the Lord's. To be protected by this battle-

142

tested shell of God's manifested grace and mercy is my need. It is the hard shell that can never fail its wearer.

Lynwood Jacobs

April 19, 1976

UNITED IN LOVE

Printed in <u>Zion's Landmark</u>

November, 1974

Dear Brother Mewborn,

While I was in North Carolina, I tried to describe the unity of love, doctrine and practice that God has granted to the churches here in our three Associations, the South Louisiana, Union and Primitive Baptist of Texas. I thank God that you were enabled to come to be with us during the Primitive Association at Jasper, Texas, to see and to share the indescribable joy and peace we are having in our churches.

The Psalmist described my present feelings: "Behold, how good and how pleasant it is for brethren to dwell together in unity! It is like the precious ointment upon the head, that ran down upon the beard, even Aaron's beard: that went down to the skirts of his garments: As the dew of Hermon, and as the dew that descended upon the mountains of Zion, for there the Lord commanded the blessing, even life for evermore." (Psalm 133)

When Christ is in the heart of His people, and the dew of sound doctrine seasoned with that love descends upon a meeting of Old Baptists, what greater blessing is there in this life? Every heart with one accord feels that He is a wonderful God. It is a sweet taste of that which is to come, even life for evermore.

Petty differences are carried away in the joy of His love. Even the few among us who weren't satisfied unless their wagging tongues were chewing on some devilish morsel of contention, seem to be gone. God, in His infinite wisdom, has appointed our Elders to know that each in nature is vain. He has blessed us to have a desire to walk as servants of the church and not as masters over God's heritage. We are blessed with a desire to walk arm in arm following Christ, and not to follow any man, or be followed by man.

To me there is no more evil spirit turned loose in the church than an Elder or group of Elders who are seeking followers. Such are accursed of Christ, and those who follow them are cursed, for cursed is the man that trusteth in man and maketh flesh his arm. The true church follows Christ, and another they will not follow.

In times past, a few have split off and devoured, then turned and devoured one another. My prayer is that Almighty God will spare us this evil spirit. It is His church, and she is in His keeping now as it has ever been. Thanks be to God that He has given us a season free of this guile. May He bless us to follow Christ, to love one another, and to manifest that love. May He keep His servants humble before God and the church. May brethren be blessed to follow that which is good—Christ, and not follow anyone caught up in the vanity of his own mind, thinking himself to be something when he is nothing.

The church has never had, wanted, or needed but one preacher and that is Christ. Any man who is convinced that he is a preacher is in trouble and everyone around him. He is exalted and shall be abased. I tell the young Elders in my correspondence that I have absolutely no confidence in them, or in myself. But, I stand in awe of the God they are made to declare, and I hope I am made to declare.

I hope that I am thankful to God for the wonderful, precious gifts of preaching that He has given us. However,

145

I am also thankful, I hope that I am blessed to worship the giver of every good and perfect gift, and not the gift.

One of the things I am made to continually ask for is that God will bless me not to set one gift above another, or one brother or sister above another. "But if ye have respect to persons, ye commit sin, and are convinced of the law as transgressors." (James 2:9) What a great blessing it is when we can rejoice equally with the frightened and stumbling beginner or the able and gifted Old Soldier of the Cross.

By and large, our young Elders have been nurtured in love as they have grown in Grace and the knowledge of our Lord and Saviour Jesus Christ. How blessed it is and how comforting it has been to them! When they stumbled, God picked them up. When they went to the top of Mount Zion, God carried them there. They are all God's precious handiwork, and each is a living miracle to me, as they must be to you, after having visited in their midst.

I hope that I shall ever be thankful for the love, and tender regard that I believe God has given me for Brother U. V. Wallace, Brother Carl DuBose, and Brother Neal Luce. I hope they have some regard for this unworthy one who had the unworthy privilege, I feel, of laying hands on each one as they were ordained to the work of a servant.

Elder C. U. Landers and Elder Cecil Jacobs are special to my soul, for each one was present to lay hands on me as I was ordained to the work, I hope, of a servant. Dear Brother, you and Elder Walter Wilson, along with the Elders in each of your correspondence have the same good report with us. Also, the precious brethren in Alabama and Florida.

I am amazed at Israel's God, how good He can be to His church in blessings. It is indescribable. May He ever bless us to look to Him as the Author and Finisher of our faith, and as the Shepherd and Bishop of our souls.

A friend, I hope,

Lynwood Jacobs

November 5, 1974

PROPHETS AND PASTORS

Published in <u>Zion's Landmark</u>

May, 1975

"And He gave some, Apostles; and some, prophets; and some, evangelists; and some pastors and teachers." (Eph. 4:11)

Sister Grace Jefferson of Lake Isabella, California, has asked me to write my thoughts on the gifts mentioned in the above scripture, "that is, if God sees fit to lead your mind to write on it." Our beloved sister indicates in this statement that God has taught her, as He has taught me, I trust, that all edifying thoughts must come from Him.

God in His infinite wisdom and perfection has ordained all things needful for the perfecting of the Saints in every age. (See Eph. 4:12.) "He is before all things, and by Him all things consist." (Col. 1:17) The Apostle James tells us that every good and perfect gift is of God. "Every good gift and every perfect gift is from above, and cometh down from the Father of lights, with whom is no variableness, neither shadow of turning." (James 1:17) I believe that the good gifts are the natural gifts that God has ordained for elect and non-elect alike. I believe the perfect gifts are the spiritual gifts that God has ordained for the elect only.

Spiritual gifts are given to fulfill His declared purposes. "This people have I formed for myself, they shall shew forth my praise." (Isa. 43:21) Not only do God's elect shew forth His praise, they also glorify God in Spirit and in Truth." ...bring my sons from far, and my daughters from the ends of the earth; Even every one that is called by My name: for I have created Him for My glory, I have formed him; yea, I have made him." (Isa. 43:6, 7) "For all things are for your sakes, that the abundant grace might through the thanksgiving of many, rebound to the glory of God." (II Cor. 4:5)

The word **Apostle** means "one sent forth." The Apostles were chosen men of God sent forth unto the lost sheep of the house of Israel and unto the Gentiles of their day, who were ordained unto eternal life. (See John 6:70, Acts 13:48 and 22:21.) The work of the Apostles is set forth in this commission of Christ to the Apostle Paul, "To open their eyes, and to turn them from darkness unto light, and from the power of Satan unto God, that they may receive forgiveness of sins, and inheritance among them which are sanctified by faith that is in me." (Acts 26:18) To carry out this charge, these chosen men of God received the greatest power from on high that God has ever given to a group of contemporaries. (Mark 16:17, 18)

I believe the Apostle Paul, as the apostle to the Gentiles, received the greatest diversity of spiritual gifts ever given to any member of the body of Christ, except the Head. He was gifted in faith, hope, charity, prayer, preaching, teaching, writing, healing, humility, wisdom, knowledge, understanding, working of miracles, speaking in tongues (other languages), interpreting tongues, discerning of Spirits, etc. He was set forth by God as a great ensample to the church. (Phil. 3:17)

The Apostle Paul endured much suffering and hardship, and each time he was blessed of God to press on to the mark of the prize of the high calling of God in Christ Jesus. "Of the Jews five times received I forty stripes save one. Thrice was I beaten with rods, once was I stoned, thrice I suffered shipwreck, a night and a day I have been in the deep; in perils of robbers, in perils by mine own countrymen, in perils by the heathen, in perils in the city….In weariness and painfulness, in watchings often, in hunger and thirst, in fastings often, in cold and nakedness." (II Cor. 11:25-27) I am amazed at the effrontery of the pompous, pampered and egotistical clergy of this day, who sit in their beautifully appointed offices, in their great brick and glass edifices, and set themselves above this blessed Apostle of God who suffered so much for the church' sake. There has been none since his day who has been given the great diversity of Spiritual gifts that God gave to him, to my knowledge.

I believe that eleven of the original Apostles (Matt. 10:12) plus the Apostle Paul are the twelve spoken of in Rev. 21:14, "And the wall of the city had twelve foundations, and in them the names of the twelve apostles of the Lamb." Judas Iscariot's bishopric was taken by another as prophesied, "Let his days be few; and let another take his office." (Psalm 109:8) The eleven remaining Apostles chose Matthias by lot to take Judas' place, but I believe God chose Saul of Tarsus (Paul) to be the twelfth Apostle before the foundation of the world. (Gal. 1:1)

The Bible says that the Spirit divides to every man severally as He will. (I Cor. 12:11) This scripture has a twofold meaning to me. God may give to one servant a diversity of gifts as He did to the Apostles. Or He may send out words by a servant that may have different spiritual effects. The same words may be teaching to one hearer or deeply inspirational to another and have little effect on a third. Ears hear, eyes see, and hearts understand as they are gifted by God. (Matt. 13:16) His doctrine astonishes. It is with power. (Luke 9:32) It accomplishes that whereunto He sends it. "So shall my word be that goeth forth out of my mouth: it shall not return unto me void, but it shall accomplish that which I please, and it shall prosper in the thing whereto I sent it." (Isa. 55:11). God creates the fruit of the lips that brings forth good tidings and great joy in the church in every age. (Isa. 57:19)

Prophecy is a declaration of that which is to come. In olden times Holy men of God spake as they were moved by the Holy Ghost. (II Peter 1:21) I believe that the work of the prophets has ended. Three scriptures tell us that the law and prophets have ended; that a greater than the prophets has come; that He has replaced prophecy, and that further active or new prophecy is not needful for the church. Christ said, "The law and the prophets were until John; since that time, the kingdom of God is preached…" (Luke 16:16) In his letter to the Hebrews, the Apostle wrote, "God, who at sundry times and in divers manners spake in time past unto the fathers by the prophets, Hath in these last days spoken unto us by His Son…" (Heb. 1:1, 2) Christ told the apostles, "It is not for you to know the times or the seasons which the Father hath put in His own power." (Acts 1:7)

When one is inspired to speak about, or write about the prophetic promises of God contained in the Bible, this is enough for the church. The believing children of God have been promised Eternal Life through the Holy will of God, and He will raise them up at the Last Day. (John 6:40) Christ prophesied that He would come again, "…and receive you unto myself; that where I am, there ye may be also." (John 14:3) The place "where I am" is far above all heavens (Eph. 4:10) where He dwells in the presence of the God and Father of all those that Christ called "His brethren." (John 20:17) He has suffered, bled, and died, but now has been glorified with the glory He had with the

151

Father before the world was. (John 17:5) Christ has given His bride the same glory which God gave to Him, that the bride may be one with herself, her Husband, and her God. (John (17:22, 23) When the bride is of age, all things have been prepared for the wedding. The veil of the law has been removed by her Husband. The wedding gown of His righteousness is prepared. Her love is now in flower, but the full aroma of her love is not yet equal to Her husband's. When the love in each part of the bride is finally totaled, I believe her love will equal her Husband's love when He comes again and bears her in His Everlasting arms across the portal of Glory into the Home that shall never end.

I believe that God does reveal unto His children certain events that are coming to pass, but these are for the individual. They are God's way of lifting up and casting down, of teaching and revealing, that He might shew forth His grace and power.

Those who are blessed to speak in types and shadows from the Old Testament are not prophets. Their hearts, minds, and souls are so filled with His presence that they see Christ in everything they read in the Old Book. They see Him in the Tree of Life, or in Joseph as a great deliverer, or maybe in Isaac about to be offered as a sacrifice unto God. I love to hear brethren speak who are gifted in this field.

I don't believe that those who are enabled or blessed to delve into the beauty of the Book of Revelation are prophets. Their hopes are centered in the prophetic promises of God contained therein. This book was not given to the church to speculate on the times and seasons, which God has put in His own power. It was given to the Church for an understanding that must come through the same Spirit that inspired the Apostle John to see and to write that which was revealed. (Rev. 1:10) I believe there is a greater simplicity in the words of this revelation than I have ever been given to understand, a simplicity that is in Christ Jesus our Lord. (See II Cor. 11:3.)

The words **evangelist** and **gospel** both mean good tidings. I believe that the Apostle Paul used the word **evangelist** in reference to the writers of the four Gospels. Each of their memoirs of the life of Christ is referred to as "The Gospel According to Matthew, or Mark, or Luke, or John." These four writers were the true evangelists. Using this term to describe someone who goes around holding "revivals" is, to say the least, a misnomer.

Inspired speaking or writing that comes from, or is in agreement with, the four gospels is evangelical. Every book in the New Testament is in strictest accord with the four gospels and are evangelical in this respect. Thus, all the doctrines taught in the New Testament are good tidings to the church. The doctrines of salvation by God's Grace, His Election, and Predestination, original sin, and the principles of the doctrine of Christ are all in harmony with and are shown in the New Testament.

The doctrines of salvation by man's work, man's free will, man's acceptance of Christ rather than being made acceptable in Christ, man's ability to "born himself" again, and man's innate ability to know the things of the Spirit of God without possessing the Spirit of God are all the commandments of men. (Matt. 15:8, 9) Since these doctrines sell, some modern groups have cast aside the King James Version of the Bible, and have written their own private interpretations of the New Testament that has this mish-mash woven throughout. These "living bibles" are living only to those who are alive to the world, but dead indeed unto the God of this Universe. I am in accord with Elder U. V. Wallace who said, "I'm glad they have their own bible, maybe they'll leave ours alone."

The word **pastor** means to pasture or feed. Christ commanded Peter to feed His lambs and sheep. The great questions then are: What is food for the church and from whence does it come? I have been made to believe that the only spiritual food the church has ever needed is TRUTH. Since Christ is the very essence of the Truth, one must have the spirit of Christ to bring forth spiritual food for the church. In the very purest sense, He is the only pastor the church has ever had, needed, or wanted. Sometimes I am caught up in the vanity of my own mind in wanting to preach or teach God's people the Truth. I had to learn through experience that this is impossible with man. Every word of Truth that has ever been uttered or that shall ever be spoken was ordained in God's Holy will and purpose before the world began. His Spirit creates the fruit of the lips which are the only sacrifices acceptable unto Almighty God. "By Him therefore let us offer the sacrifice of praise to God continually, that is, the fruit of our lips giving thanks to His name." (Heb. 14:15) If we were blessed to fulfill this scripture to a jot and tittle, there would be no time in the church for anything but the expressions of thanks to His Holy name.

God alone knows the spiritual needs of His people, and He alone can fulfill those needs. When Christ commanded Peter to feed His lambs and sheep, this was a commandment with power. The Apostles received power from on high to keep His commandments. "And behold, I send the promise of my Father unto you: but tarry ye in the city of Jerusalem, until ye be endued with power from on high." (Luke 24:49)

Just as Christ is the only pastor the church has, so is He the only teacher. One of the principles of the new covenant written in His blood is this: "And they shall not teach every man his neighbor, and every man his brother, saying, know the Lord: for all shall know me, from the least to the greatest." (Heb.8:11) Prophecy foretold how. "And all thy children shall be taught of the Lord, and great shall be the peace of thy children." (Isa. 54:13) Christ referred to this very scripture, "It is written in the prophets, and they shall be all taught of God. Every man therefore that hath heard and hath learned of the Father, cometh unto me." (John 6:45)

The Apostle Paul sums up teaching in this way. "...even so the things of God knoweth no man, but the spirit of God. Which things also we speak, not in the words which man's wisdom teacheth, but which the Holy Ghost teacheth..." (I Cor. 2:11, 13) It is not by the spirit of the world that we speak or receive the things of God, but by the Spirit of God, "Now we have received, not the spirit of the world, but the Spirit which is of God; that we might know the things that are FREELY given us of God." (I Cor. 2:12) This is our hope, that we have received these things which are of God.

"Now there are diversities of Gifts, but the same Spirit. And there are differences of administration, but the same Lord. And there are diversities of operations, but it is the same Lord which worketh all in all." (I Cor. 12:4-6) The church is His. He has supplied her every need in every age. "Unto Him be glory in the church by Christ Jesus throughout all ages, world without end. Amen." (Eph. 3:21)

Lynwood Jacobs

March 6, 1975

FEAR NOT

Fear not, little flock; for it is your Father's good pleasure to give you the Kingdom. (Luke 12:32) These words do not mean to fear not God who has the power to destroy both soul and body in hell. These words mean fear not them that can destroy the body, which they cannot do, except by the ordained will of God. (See Matt. 10:28.) These words can mean: My children, be not afraid of the reproach of men or their reviling against words of praise and adoration that come forth from a Spirit filled heart. (See Isa. 51:7.) David, be not afraid of Goliath. Moses, tell the children of Israel to fear not Pharaoh and his army, but to stand still and see the salvation of the Lord. (See Ex. 14:13.) May we be blessed to stand still in the liberty wherewith Christ has made His people free, and be not entangled again in that yoke of bondage which neither we nor our forefathers were able to bear. May God's love bind us to Him, to His precious Son, and to one another. Perfect love casts out fear!

Fear thee not; for I am with thee: be not dismayed; for I am thy God: I will strengthen thee; yea, I will help thee; yea. I will uphold thee with the right hand of my righteousness. (Isa .41:10) The Saints of God trust in His strength and not their own. They hope for the imputed righteousness of God through Jesus Christ knowing that their own righteousness is but as a filthy rag. They believe that God made His Son, who knew no sin, to be sin for them that they might be made the righteousness of God in Him. They believe that their part in the Kingdom was assured when God chose them in Christ Jesus before the foundation of the world. (See Eph. 1:4.)

And the angel said unto them, Fear not: for, behold, I bring you good tidings of great joy, which shall be to all the people. For unto you is born this day in the city of David a Saviour, which is Christ the Lord. (Luke 2:10, 11) As the angel spoke these words to the shepherds in the field, the glory of the Lord shown round about them. The message to them has gone out to His Saints in all stages of time. Fear not, ye Saints of God. Christ the Lord has arrived from eternity to prepare His brethren for their eternal home.

Fear not ye: for I know ye seek Jesus, which was crucified. He is not here: for He is risen, as He said. Come see the place where the Lord lay. (Matt. 28:5, 6) These words were spoken by an angel of God unto the women who came to His grave. May that same messenger of God bear witness unto each one of us that He is risen, that He is alive, that He has saved His people from their sins. When we are filled with a blessed hope that we were chosen to be in that number, then we fear not.

Fear not: for I am with thee: I will bring thy seed from the east, and gather thee from the west; I will say to the north, Give up; and to the south, Keep not back; bring my sons from far, and my daughters from the ends of the earth; even every one that is called by my name: for I have created him for my glory, I have formed him; yea, I have made him. (Isa. 43:5-7) These words are for His children, those that God has created for His glory, those that shall show forth His praise, not only in this life, but also in that eternal home that shall never end. God is with them now, wherever they are, and He will never leave them nor forsake them. He has loved His creation with everlasting love and with loving kindness He draws them unto Himself at His appointed time.

Fear not, Abraham and Sarah, for God has wrought a great work in thee. Fear not, thou worm Jacob and ye men of

Israel for God has helped thee sayeth thy redeemer, the Holy One of Israel. The Lord that created thee, O Jacob, and He that formed thee, O Israel, says, Fear not, for I have redeemed thee, I have called thee by thy name; thou art mine. (See Isa.43:1.) Saved by God's grace, redeemed by Christ's blood out of every nation and people, and called out of nature's darkness into His marvelous light, what more do we need if we are His children? Fear not!

Lynwood Jacobs

February 2008

THY KINGDOM COME

"All Thy works shall praise Thee, O Lord; and Thy saints shall bless Thee. They shall speak of the glory of Thy kingdom, and talk of Thy power; To make known to the sons of men His mighty acts, and the glorious majesty of His kingdom. Thy kingdom and Thy dominion endureth throughout all generations." (Psalms 145:10-13)

These beautiful words of the psalmist have inspired the hearts of saints in every generation. Faithful Abraham was not the only one to seek for a city with foundation, whose builder and maker is God. (See Heb. 11:10.) By the same God-given faith the psalmists and many in this day look for that kingdom where they hope to see the King in His beauty, and behold the land that is very far off. (See Is. 33:17.)

This everlasting Kingdom of God in all its sanctified glory is the promise to every saint that has been given to praise God in spirit and in truth. "Fear not, little flock; for it is your Father's good pleasure to give you the kingdom." (Luke 12:32) "But the hour cometh, and now is when the true worshippers shall worship the Father in spirit and in truth..." (John 4:23)

The mighty acts of the Triune Godhead are administering an entrance into this glorious kingdom for every saint. The Apostle Peter said, "For so an entrance shall be ministered unto you abundantly into the everlasting kingdom of our Lord and Saviour Jesus Christ." (II Peter 1:11)

As the sainted subjects are being fitted for that kingdom, they have their hopes laid only on the mighty works of God. The psalmist testified, "I will speak of the glorious honor of thy majesty, and of Thy wondrous works." (Psalm 145:5) They ascribe salvation to God even as that innumerable host that the Apostle John beheld, "After this I beheld, and lo, a great multitude, which no man could number, of all nations, and kindred, and people, and tongues, stood before the throne, and before the Lamb, clothed with white robes, and palms in their hands; and cried with a loud voice, saying, Salvation to our God which sitteth upon the throne, and unto the Lamb." (Rev. 7:9-10)

They say, "Amen" with those that declare, "...Blessing, and glory, and wisdom, and thanksgiving and honour, and power, and might, be unto our God forever. Amen." (Rev. 7:12)

When one of His disciples said unto Him, "Lord, teach us to pray," Christ answered him, thusly, "When ye pray, say, Our Father which art in heaven, Hallowed be Thy name, Thy kingdom come..." (Luke 11:12) As God's will unravels on the pages of time, His kingdom must come for those He has loved and drawn with an everlasting love," "Yes, I have loved thee with an everlasting love—therefore, with loving kindness have I drawn thee." (Jer. 31:3)

The angel Gabriel said unto Mary, "...And He shall reign over the house of Jacob forever; and of His kingdom there shall be no end." (Luke 1:33) Only in Christ, the Sanctifier, do His sanctified brethren possess this kingdom which is His inheritance to share with those who are all of one with Him. "For both He that sanctifieth, and they who are sanctified are all of one; for which cause He is not ashamed to call them brethren." (Heb. 2:11) "In whom also we have an inheritance, being predestinated according to the purpose of Him who worketh all things after the council of His own will." (Eph. 1:11)

The Apostle Peter laid out the hope of this heavenly inheritance for every saint begotten of and kept by the power of God. "Blessed be the God and Father of our Lord Jesus Christ, which according to His abundant mercy hath begotten us again unto a lively hope by the resurrection of Jesus Christ from the dead, to an inheritance incorruptible, and undefiled, and that fadeth not away, reserved in heaven for you who are kept by the power of God through faith unto salvation ready to be ready to be revealed in the last time." (I Peter 1:3-5) Prophecy declared some names of the Ruler of this enduring Kingdom. It says that though He was to be manifest upon the earth, yet His goings forth were from everlasting. "For unto us a child is born, unto us a Son is given: and the government shall be upon His shoulder: and His name shall be called Wonderful, Councilor, The mighty God, The everlasting Father, The Prince of Peace." (Isa. 9:6) "But thou Bethlehem Ephratah, though thou be little among the thousands of Judah, yet out of thee shall He come forth unto me that is to be ruler in Israel; whose goings forth have been from of old, from everlasting." (Mica 5:2)

As the King walked the face of this earth in a body prepared for Him by God, He said, "My kingdom is not of this world." (John 18:36) He said, also, "The Kingdom of God is within you." (Luke 17:21) This inward kingdom which is not of this world is in those who are not of the world, even as He is not of the world. "They are not of the world, even as I am not of the world." (John 17:16) This inward kingdom is a seal of promise of that world which is to come and is not beholden to death, for its King has, through death, destroyed him that had the power of death. (See Heb. 2:14-15.)

This inward kingdom breaks in pieces and consumes all other kingdoms, and it shall stand forever. (See Dan. 2:4.) It is invisible, yet the light of the body is the eye; therefore when thine eye is single, the whole body also is full of light…" (Luke 11:34)

This inward kingdom cannot be seen in others nor light shine forth from it until one is born again. "Except a man be born again he cannot see the Kingdom of God." (John 3:3) This new birth makes the eye single with love, since the planting of God's seed of love in a sinner's heart is the new birth with power. So this inward kingdom is one of love. It is not meat and drink, but righteousness and peace and joy in the Holy Spirit. (See Rom. 14:17.)

In this time world the saints have this treasure (kingdom) in earthen vessels, but for the world to come they must put on that tabernacle not made with hands, eternal in the heavens. "For God, who commanded the light to shine out of darkness, hath shined in our hearts, to give the light of the knowledge of the glory of God in the face of Jesus Christ. But we have this treasure in earthen vessels, that the excellency of the power may be of God, and not of us." (II Cor. 4:6-7) "For we know that if the earthly house of this our tabernacle were dissolved, we have a building of God, an house not made with hands, eternal in the heavens." (II Cor. 5:11)

On the morning of the resurrection when Christ shall have raised their vile bodies and fashioned them like unto His glorious body, the saints will be clothed upon with that house not made with hands, eternal in the heavens. (See Phil. 3:21.) Then shall the righteous shine forth in the Kingdom of their Father (Matt. 13:43) With that inward kingdom now cloaked in a glorified tabernacle they shall live forever in that heavenly kingdom that shall never end, eternal in the heavens. When they have been there ten thousand years, bright shining as the sun, they've no less days to sing God's praise than when they've first begun. (See Lloyd's Hymn, 355.)

This ingathering will be then, even as it is now, the work of God. "Fear not, for I am with thee: I will bring thy seed from the east, and gather thee from the west: I will say to the north, Give up; and to the south, Keep not back: bring My sons from far, and My daughters from the ends of the earth, Even every one that is called by My name; for I have created Him for my glory, I have formed him: yea, I have made him." (Isa. 43:5-7)

The Apostle Paul tells us that in this life the saints have borne the image of the earthy, but in the life to come they shall bear the image of the heavenly. "As we have borne the image of the earthy, we shall also bear the image of the heavenly. If in this life only we have hope in Christ, we are of all men most miserable." (I Cor. 15:49, 19)

What a wonderful hope it is to believe that a way has been administered for God's people into that eternal Kingdom. That way is Christ. He has promised to return again, and receive His people unto Himself, that where He is now, there may they be also. (See John 14:1-3.)

What a wonderful trust has been given to God's people, They trust in His works, His power, His salvation, His resurrection and His way. "Trust in the Lord with all thine heart; and lean not unto thine own understanding. In all thy ways acknowledge Him, and He shall direct thy paths." (Psalm 2:5-6)

Sometimes the path may seem dim, and the journey painful, wearisome and hopeless. Yet, even this is not to be compared to the glory that shall be revealed in those that love God. When they see Him as they are seen, know Him as they are known, only then will they be truly satisfied. "As for me, I will behold thy face in righteousness: I shall be satisfied when I awake with thy likeness." (Psalm 17:15)

This is written in the hope that the glorious words from the 145th Psalm used as an introduction will find a place in the hearts of the present generation, "One generation shall praise Thy works to another, and shall declare Thy mighty works." (Psalm 145:4)

All of God's works praise Him. The blessed saints do bless Him. They speak of the glory of His Kingdom and talk of His power. He has made known to them His mighty acts. They have received the earnest of the inheritance by promise of the glorious majesty of His Kingdom. They have the surety that His Kingdome and dominion endureth forever. Their hope is rested on the promise that prayer to God is answered, when it comes from a heart crying, "Thy Kingdom come."

Lynwood Jacobs

January 19, 1976

FATALISM AND PREDESTINATION

February 1973

Dear Brother Adams,

Maybe I should wait for the conclusion of the article on
Fatalism which was begun in the December 1, 1972, issue
of Zion's Landmark, but I have some thoughts on the
subject which I want to write down while they are fresh on
my mind, God Willing. I trust these thoughts are in
harmony with the complete article.

First, here are some definitions. Fatalism is the belief that
man's destiny is determined by fate. Predestination is the
belief that man's destiny was determined by God. Absolute
predestination is the belief that man's destiny and all
things, whether visible or invisible, were determined by
God who worketh all things after the council of His own
will.

The Doctrine of Absolute Predestination was given to the
church by an absolute God. It was not given to the world.
This doctrine is called Fatalism by a pseudo religious world
who knows not God, so they have substituted a vague term
"fate" that is about as elusive as their begging, blind, and
unsettled God. There are those who say God predestinated
the good things, such as eternal life, but none of the bad.
This last group is the most perplexing of all to me, and here
is why. If a man believes in the absolute sovereignty of
God, I know where he stands. If a man believes in the
doctrine of the free will of man, I know where he stands.
But when a man tries to mix the two, he is trying to pawn
off on me a half-sheep, half-goat, half-elect, half-non-elect,
half-works, half-grace, part this, part that, mish-mash that
which would confuse the devil, himself.

God is God, blessed forevermore. He only has the divine attributes of Himself. To me, this is what the Doctrine of Absolute Predestination tells the church. His attributes are unchangeable and scripture plus experience reveals some of them to the church—not the world. The world cannot receive the Spirit of Truth by whom God reveals Himself, neither His attributes which are revealed to each one of His beloved children.

I will not try to quote scripture verbatim to cover my thoughts on the attributes of God. If we are children of God, we have learned concerning His attributes by experience. The precious scriptures bear witness with our witness which is within. God has all power in heaven and in earth. He has power over all flesh. He is love and gives this love to His people. He hates with a perfect hatred. He chooses and rejects; He works and none can stay His hand; His works are perfect.

God gives men to believe on Him through the workings of His mighty power. He has created all things for Himself—without Him was not anything made that was made. He is here and there, even where the morning stars sing together. He is omnipresent—everywhere present. He is able to do exceeding abundantly above all that we ask or think through His power that worketh in us. God is beloved and worthy to receive glory and honor and praise from His people. He is wonderful, councilor, and a father of His children. He is to the church wisdom, righteousness, sanctification, and redemption. He is the Shepherd and Bishop of our soul, the Author and Finisher of our faith and salvation; yea, our all in all. Holy, just, and perfect in all His ways is our God. He is truth, the resurrection, our life and our way if so be that the Spirit of God dwell in us—if so be He has given us to drink of the river of the water of

Life freely, to taste the Good Word of God and the power of the world to come.

He said that His thoughts are higher above our thoughts and His ways higher than our ways as the heavens are above the earth. God made two great lights, the greater light to shine by day and the lesser light to shine by night. He also made the stars. How infinite is our God! How incomprehensible is the Lord of this universe by feeble sense alone.

Above all else, the divine attribute of God which makes this sinner cry out in hope is that He is a God of mercy. Mercy, yea, Divine Mercies of God. How wonderful that He is a God of Mercy. Maybe, just maybe, my case is not hopeless. Oh God, be merciful to my unrighteousness and my sins and inequities remember against me no more, forever.

Is it just possible that I can awake in His likeness and be satisfied? Will He bless me to praise Him with a perfect praise in that bright land that shall never end? Will He bless me to love Him to the very depths of my soul; to see Him as He is, and to behold His eternal glory when He comes again to receive you unto Himself that where He is there may you be also? I do not know the answer to these questions, but whether they be yes or no, God is God and perfect in all His judgments.

In conclusion, Brother Adams, the Doctrine of Absolute Predestination needs no defending. The dead can't hear it, and living do believe it already. We can only hope that God will bless us to declare it to His people. This doctrine that is so strange to the natural man is the foundation of the truth, and the truth is as eternal, perfect, and unchangeable as God. I am not afraid to declare that God predestinated the entrance of sin into the world just because sin exists. If

167

God had not had a holy and divine purpose in sin, He would have left out the devil, vanity, temptation, and the weakness which is ours in the flesh. But it pleased Him to create the bride of Christ, weak in the flesh, that she might receive strength, and all things, through her precious Husband, the Lamb of God, to whom be glory both now and forevermore.

We desire to see you and Sister Adams again so much, because we believe that a wonderful God brought you to us in love here in Texas.

Lynwood Jacobs

Written December 22, 1972

GEMS 1

Gems are verses of scripture that alone present a powerful message to believers. One of the earliest examples is Genesis 4:26. "And to Seth, to him also there was born a son; and he called his name Enos: then men began to call upon the name of the Lord." Seth was a son of Adam. This establishes the fact that men began to worship God from the beginning of humanity. God has ever had witnesses among men on earth to praise, honor, and glorify him. They are called a remnant according to the election of grace.

Rev. 4:10. "Thou art worthy, O Lord, to receive glory, honor, and power: for thou hast created all things, and for thy pleasure they are and were created." This revelation to John made thousands of years after men began to call upon the name of the Lord, explain the purpose of God's creation--that it is all for his pleasure. Those blessed to be manifested members of His family are given a peace that passes all human understanding by such scriptures as this. Their God is the God of creation of life, of immortality, of grace and mercy, of unending power and glory, of things seen and unseen, of nations and stars, of light and darkness both natural and spiritual, of elect and nonelect, of saints and wicked, of blessings and curses, of sight and blindness, and, yes, of innumerable things and events not mentioned here. Certainly HE is worthy to receive glory, honor and power from his family, the family of God.

Isa. 33:17. "Thine eyes shall see the king in his beauty: they shall behold the land that is very far off." No greater promise has ever been made to his Saints, except the promise of Christ as Saviour. No greater event will ever occur to them than when they first behold Him, the King of Kings, the everlasting God, and to see Him as He is when they go home to dwell in that beautiful land that is very far off. That life and immortality that Christ brought to light through the gospel of peace will now be manifest in its fullness, no more to be diluted by the trappings of the flesh.

Isa. 43:21. "This people have I formed for myself; they shall shew forth my praise." The people of God have no confidence in the arm of flesh. They worship God in Spirit and in Truth, the only way he can be worshipped. In their formation they are gifted with the Holy Ghost, a spirit of wisdom and revelation of the divine attributes and purposes of God. This Holy Spirit alone prepares them for that home that is very far off, where they will praise him forever with a perfect praise that shall never end. Isaiah was one of the holy men of old who wrote as they were moved by the Spirit of God, often to write as though it was God himself speaking. In the truest sense, it was God speaking through the prophets.

Prov. 8:22, 23. "The Lord possessed me in the beginning of his way, before his works of old. I was set up from everlasting, from the beginning, or ever the earth was." There is no way for the natural man to conceive of the God of this universe, nor conceive of one who was with God when there was no earth, no mountains, no water, no fields, nor dust of the ground. The creation was yet only in the mind and purpose of God's holy will. To present this true God, or his Son, as some nice old grandfatherly figure who loves everybody, and who wants and wishes, and will-if-you-let-him is the most horrible abomination on earth, to me.

Isa. 7:14. "Therefore the Lord himself shall give you a sign; Behold, a virgin shall conceive, and bear a son, and shall call his name Immanuel." The word Immanuel means

GOD WITH US. This great prophecy occurred hundreds of years before the coming of Christ to earth. It must have brought scorn to Isaiah from nonbelievers, as well as joy to those who believed. For years, until his birth of the Virgin Mary, great was the number of young virgins who wanted to be the one to be the mother of Christ. There are those today of the same mind, still denying his birth.

Heb. 7:19. "For the law made nothing perfect, but the bringing in of a better hope did, by the which we draw nigh unto God." The law was, and is perfect for the purpose it was created, even the law written on tables of stone. That law shows our imperfections because none has ever kept them to perfection except Christ. Being sinners, we look to the God of hope, who alone can fill us with all joy and peace in believing, that we may abound in hope through the power in the gift of the Holy Ghost. This gift imparts to our heart and mind the perfect law of liberty, the law of the Spirit of Life in Christ, the law of love that binds the saints to one another, and to Christ, and through him to God. We are drawn unto God by hope, through faith, and that not of ourselves, they are a gift of God.

Eze. 36:26, 27. "A new heart also will I give you, and a new spirit will I put within you; and I will take away the stony heart out of your flesh, and I will give you an heart of flesh. And I will put my spirit within you, and cause you to walk in my statutes, and ye shall keep my judgments, and do them." When one is born again of the Holy Spirit, they walk in love, and go with thankful hearts to God for the saving grace in Christ Jesus. They walk in a new path ordained for them by God before the world began. It is the way of righteousness that leads unto life everlasting. It is the way of thankfulness to God, the way of joy, peace, humility, and compassion. Above all else, it is the way that leads to God and Christ.

Isa. 43:11. "I, even I, am the Lord; and beside me there is no saviour." No private interpretation of other scriptures can change the fact that Jesus Christ is the only saviour of men, and the souls of men. He knows those whose names are in the Book of Life, because his Father wrote the Book and Christ co-signed it. He agreed with his father to die on the cross to remove the sins of his brethren, before Adam was formed from the dust of the earth. The gift of the Holy Ghost makes them manifested children of the King. Only God through Christ bestows eternal life to his Saints. Anyone saying they have saved a soul deceives themselves, and the Truth is not in them. When some the Apostle Paul thought he had saved turned against him, this made him to understand that he was not the saviour of God's children. When God saves, they are saved forever.

Lynwood Jacobs

2012

GEMS 2

Gems are verses of scripture that alone present a powerful message to believers.

Only a part of some verses of Scripture are profound statements of the truth. A good example is Acts 13:48. "And when the Gentiles heard this, they were glad, and glorified the word of God, AND AS MANY AS WERE ORDAINED TO ETERNAL LIFE BELIEVED." This has not changed with time. Today, as then, as many as were ordained to eternal life by almighty God believe, and no one else! Paul and Barnabas had just turned to the Gentiles because the Jews did not believe in the risen Christ. The Apostle brought joy and gladness to those Gentiles, both then and now, who were before ordained of God to believe the truth. Their names are in the Book of Life. They were chosen in Christ before the world began.

Acts 2:39. "For the promise is to you, and to your children, and to all that are far off, EVEN AS MANY AS THE LORD OUR GOD SHALL CALL. These words by the Apostle Peter say explicitly that the promise of salvation is to those that God calls out of darkness, into the glorious liberty of the children of God. God calls with a holy calling, not according to our works, but according to his purpose and grace, given us in Christ Jesus before the world began. God calls with power, a direct spiritual awakening to his child with no intermediary needed. His amazing grace fills his children with praises to God and their saviour Jesus Christ.

Acts 2:47. "Praising God, and having favour with all the people. AND THE LORD ADDED TO THE CHURCH DAILY SUCH AS SHOULD BE SAVED." Only God's elect that gladly received Peter's words of truth, believed and were baptized. God still adds to the church daily such as should be saved. Those that gladly receive His word are his children whose appointed time has come for revelation. That time was ordained of God before the world began. It is called the new birth, when they are born, not of the flesh, but born of God. It is the time for baptism of the Holy Ghost and with fire, when they receive that Spirit of wisdom and revelation in the knowledge of God, the eyes of their understanding being enlightened. They then begin to grow in grace and true knowledge.

I John 5:14. "And this is the confidence that we have in him, that, IF WE ASK ANYTHING ACCORDING TO HIS WILL, HE HEARETH US." This statement blesses us to understand the difference between begging and praying. If we ask God for things we don't have, this is begging. If we are thankful to God for what we have this is praying. True prayer is the fruit of our lips and heart rendering praise and thankfulness to God and his Son for our many blessings. True prayer indicates that God has reconciled us to his will, which is done in heaven and among the inhabitants of the earth. Those reconciled can say with Christ to their Father, "not my will, but thy will be done."

Heb. 8:10. "For this is the covenant I will make with the house of Israel after those days, saith the Lord: I WILL PUT MY LAWS INTO THEIR MIND, AND WRITE THEM IN THEIR HEARTS: and I will be unto them a God and they shall be unto me a people." Moses received the law to be written on tables of stone. Christ received the law to be written in the heart and mind of God's people. Thou shalt love thy God and thy neighbor, on these two laws hang all the law and the prophets. There is no "ought to" anything. You shall love when the love of God is shed

174

abroad in your heart, by the Holy Ghost which is given you of God. Then you shall walk in the way of righteousness, and perform those good works that your heavenly Father before ordained that you should walk in them.

Lynwood Jacobs

2012

GEMS 3

Gems are verses of scripture that alone present a powerful message to believers.

1 Cor. 2:14. "But the natural man receiveth not the things of the Spirit of God: for they are foolishness to him: neither can he know them, because   they are spiritually discerned." In this letter unto the church of God which was at Corinth, to them which were sanctified in Christ Jesus, and called to be saints, the Apostle Paul was blessed to separate the wheat from the chaff. He was to tell them that eye hath not seen, nor ear heard, neither hath entered into the heart of man, the things which God hath prepared for THEM THAT LOVE HIM. Why? Because God reveals them by his Spirit. Them that love him are the ones that have the love of God shed abroad in their heart by God, who first loved them. According to the manifest will of God, the spirit of man reveals only natural things, and the Spiritual things of God are foolishness to him. According to the manifest will of God, those that have his Spirit searcheth all things, yea, even the deep things of God. To say that the natural man can accept Christ as his personal saviour is foolishness.

John 17:2. "As thou hast given him power over all flesh, that he should give eternal life to as many as thou hast given him." This statement of Christ when he was talking to his Father is as plain as anything written in the scriptures. Christ has not only power over all flesh, but all power in heaven and in earth. He will have this power until he delivers up the Kingdom to God. Eternal life is a gift, and it is for those that God gave to Christ. God ordained eternal life, Christ paid for it, and the Holy Ghost makes it manifest. God glorified Christ, Christ glorified his brethren, and both Christ and his brethren glorify their Father. That is what eternal life is all about!

Heb.13:21." Make you perfect in every good work to do his will, working in you that which is well pleasing in his sight, through Jesus Christ; to whom be glory for ever and ever, Amen." Brethren, don't worry! The God of peace is the one who works in you both the will and do of his good pleasure, and you will manifest good works according to his ordained will. Christ's power is the same God given power that brought Christ from the dead through the blood of the everlasting covenant. The Saints of old did not know when they did a good work, because they asked Christ," When did we do these things?" He told them that since they had done these things unto the least of his little ones, they had done it unto him. We do not even know who his little ones are, but Christ knows them. Good works are the fruit of the Spirit, and are the outward manifestation of God's love in our heart. My 16 year old granddaughter says that the doctrine according to Lynwood 1:1 is "If true love is the source, there can't be anything wrong with it." I say, amen, and praise God that she also believes it.

John 6:44. "No man can come to me, except the Father which sent me draw him: and I will raise him up again at the last day." Further along (John 6:63) Christ gives the reason for this statement, " It is the Spirit that quickeneth; the flesh profiteth nothing: the words that I speak unto you, they are spirit, and they are life." They that are in the flesh cannot believe in God, but they are not in the flesh, but in the Spirit, if so be that the Spirit of God dwell in them. Christ said that I and my Father will take up our abode in you. When they do, your body becomes a temple of the Holy Spirit which you have received as a gift of God. When they do you become a manifested Saint of God.

177

When you are raised again on the last day the Holy Spirit which is yours, will take up its abode in your Spiritual body, and so shall you ever be a living, embodied Saint, who worships the Lord thy God forever.

Psalm 23:6. "Surely goodness and mercy shall follow me all the days of my life: and I will dwell in the house of the Lord forever." There are no more beloved words in the Bible to many than those in the 23rd Psalm. This last verse is the hope of those sanctified in Christ Jesus. What a joyous event when they can say, "Surely Christ's goodness and God's mercy has followed me all the days of my life, and I am now dwelling in the house of the Lord forever.

Lynwood Jacobs

February 2012

GEMS 4

Gems are verses of scripture that alone carry a powerful message to those that believe.

1 John 3:2. "Beloved, now are we the sons of God, and it doth not yet appear what we shall be: but we know that, when he shall appear, we shall be like him; for we shall see him as he is." Beloved, John has given us a joyful and fearful hope that we are children of God, and that we shall see him as he sees us, and be like him. He is coming back, just as he went away, to raise his brethren that are waiting to be with him. David said that his eyes would behold him, and that he would be satisfied when he awakened in his likeness. Every child of God shall behold Christ, and won't be truly satisfied until they awake in his likeness. Then the will of Christ shall be fulfilled, that his brethren be where he is now, that they might behold the glory that his Father gave to him before he created the world and all things therein.

1 Tim.1:15. "This is a faithful saying, and worthy of all acceptation, that Christ Jesus came into the world to save sinners; of whom I am chief." This is probably the most questioned scripture in the Bible, by those of us who have felt ourselves to be chief of sinners. All have sinned and come short of the glory of God. His righteousness is the only righteousness acceptable unto God. Thus Christ, who knew no sin, was made sin for his brethren that they might be made the righteousness of God in him. Man's self-righteousness has never been acceptable unto God.

Acts 1:7. "And he said to them, it is not for you to know the times or the seasons, which the Father has put in his own power:" These words spoke Christ to his disciples after his passion, when they wanted to know when he was going to set up his kingdom on earth. They evidently did not understand what he meant when he said my kingdom is not of this world, though it will be taken out of the world, and delivered up to God on the last day. These words certainly apply today when fools predict the end of the world on a certain date or time.

Heb.1:3. "who being the brightness of his glory, and the express image of his person, and upholding all things by the word of his power, when he had by himself purged our sins, sat down on the right hand of the Majesty on high:" The "who" written here is Jesus Christ. The risen Christ was the brightness of God's glory and the express image of His person. His brethren who come forth in Christ's image, will then be in the image of their Father, because God has created them in his image and after his likeness. Christ is alive at the right hand of God. He has put the sins of his brethren as far away as the east is from the west, never to be remembered against them. I hope he is waiting for a command of his Father, "Son, go bring my children home." Lord, may I be numbered in that blessed family of God.

2 Tim.2:9. "Who hath saved us, and called us with an holy calling, not according to our works, but according to his own purpose and grace, which was given us in Christ Jesus before the world began." Paul went on to say that Christ hath abolished death, and hath brought life and immortality to light through the gospel of peace. The world cries out, "Save yourself, before it is too late." God before ordained that Christ would save his brethren on an old rugged cross some two thousand years ago. There has been no more sacrifice for sin since that day. Only God through his Spirit calls his children out of darkness into his marvelous light, and saves their soul forever. It is too late to add ones name in the Book of Life.

Lynwood Jacobs

2012

GEMS 5

Gems are single verses of scripture that alone carry a powerful message to believers.

Eph. 1:4. "According as he hath chosen us in him before the foundation of the world, that we should be holy and without blame before him in love." With this statement before us, how can anyone deny the doctrine of election? The undeniable truth is that God chose his children in Christ before the world began. This letter was addressed to the Saints at Ephesus, and to the faithful in Christ Jesus, which reaches those Saints who were to follow, even to this day. Every one of them was ordained to eternal life because of God's love for his Elect. Christ took upon himself to pay for the sins of his brethren, who would be manifested in time.

Matt. 6: 10. "Thy kingdom come, Thy will be done in earth, as it is in heaven." These words from Jesus are part of what is commonly called the Lord 's Prayer. They totally refute man's free-will doctrine. Why? Because Christ knew that God's will, not HIS or OURS, is done in earth as it is in heaven. We pray from thankful hearts for God's will to be done when he has first reconciled us to his will by his Spirit.

1 Cor. 13:13. "And now abideth faith, hope, and charity, these three; but the greatest of these is charity." Faith, when worked by God's love in our heart, gives substance to the things we hope for, and is evidence of things not seen. By God's gift of faith, we hope that God, who we see not, is our heavenly Father. By faith, we hope that Christ, who we see not, is our Saviour. By faith, we hope that God has united our hearts in love with a few of his elect children here on earth. By faith, we hope to partake of that life and immortality that Christ brought to light through the gospel of peace.

John 3:5. "Jesus answered, Verily, verily, I say unto thee, Except a man be born of water (the flesh) and of the spirit, he cannot enter into the kingdom of God." If being born of water refers to water baptism by man then we have to be born three different times, born of the flesh, born of the water, and born of the Spirit. I don't believe that. Christ insisted that one has to be born again to even see the kingdom of God. In preparing his Saints for everlasting life, God ordained that they would be born of the flesh first, and then born again of the Spirit. A birth follows conception. In the first birth of the flesh, we are conceived in sin and brought forth in iniquity. In the new birth of the Spirit, we were conceived in righteousness and are brought forth free of sin. They that are in the flesh desire the things of the flesh, while they that are in the Spirit desire the things of the Spirit. The non-elect's strength is in the arm of flesh, while the elect's strength is in the arm of God, Jesus Christ.

2 Cor. 11:3. "But I fear, lest by any means, as the serpent beguiled Eve through subtilty, so your minds should be corrupted from the simplicity that is in Christ." In this letter unto the church of God at Corinth, and all the Saints at Achaia, Paul both praises and reproves them for the myriad practices, both sound and unsound, that were taking place in the days of his Apostleship. An example of folly was Simon the scorcer who attempted to buy power from Peter to give the Holy Ghost. Simon had bewitched the people until they thought he was some great one. Peter said unto Simon, "Thy money perish with thee, BECAUSE THOU HAST THOUGHT THAT THE GIFT OF GOD MAY BE PURCHASED WITH MONEY." The world is full of beguiling Simons today, and they with him are in the gall of bitterness, and in the bond of iniquity. They cry out to the deluded, send me your money, and I'll see that you go to heaven. Love one another as He loved is the simplicity in Christ Jesus. Upon this Love in his brethren, all Spiritual and everlasting events depend for manifestation.

Lynwood Jacobs

2012

GEMS 6

Gems are verses of scripture that alone have a powerful message for believers.

Dan. 12:10. "Many shall be purified, and made white, and tried; but the wicked shall do wickedly: and none of the wicked shall understand; but the wise shall understand." God created every one of the wicked, and they do wickedly. They are conceived in sin and brought forth in iniquity never to understand the things of God and Christ. That includes you, and me, and everyone that is born of the flesh. Hell is the destiny of all mankind, except for the electing grace of God. We have all sinned and come short of the glory of God. There is none good, no not one, except Jesus Christ. There is a chosen remnant on earth, according to the election of grace that are purified and made white, free from sin by the righteousness of God, imputed to them through Jesus Christ. Heaven is their destiny, though they are no more worthy in the flesh than the vilest sinner. Did God create me? Yes! Am I a sinner? Yes! And hell bound except for the grace of God. That alone makes God the creator of one convicted sinner that has a hope of eternal life. There are others.

2 Thes. 2:13. "But we are bound to give thanks always to God for you, brethren beloved of the Lord, because God hath from the beginning chosen you to salvation through sanctification of the Spirit and belief of the truth:" How great must have been Paul's joy that brought forth these words! There is no time in eternity. As far as we know, time began with the creation of this world by God, and he ordained that his children would be mortals first, created in time with a beginning and an end. When God acted, "Let us make man in our image," mankind then had its beginning.

God ordained his loved ones to be sanctified, set apart by his Spirit to believe in Christ, the Truth. Christ loved the chosen ones of God enough to come suffer their mortality, that they might have immortality through him.

2 Cor. 13:14. "The grace of the Lord Jesus Christ, and the love of God, and communion of the Holy Ghost, be with you all." What a beautiful salutation Paul used to close his letter to the church of the Thessalonicas! By his grace, Christ fills his brethren with the fruit of righteousness to the glory and praise of God. By grace they look to Christ as the author and finisher of their faith, and as the shepherd and Bishop of their souls. When God's gift of love fills ones heart, they possess the most powerful force in the world. It welds them forever to God, to Christ, and to their brethren. It blesses them through the power of the Holy Ghost, to walk in ordained paths of righteousness, and the end everlasting life.

Rom. 8:34. "Who is he that condemneth? It is Christ that died, yea rather, that is risen again, who is even at the right hand of God, who also maketh intercession for us." This letter was written to those in Rome, beloved of God, and called to be Saints. Paul was driving home the fact that Jesus Christ, then and now, is the only intercessor between man and God. He is alive! He is alive, in the presence of God, and we need him to intercede for us, and not some earth bound fake! The law condemns us, but if Christ interceded for us we cannot be condemned, because we are no longer under the law, but under grace.

Rom. 9:13. "As it is written, Jacob have I loved, but Esau have I hated." This scripture proves that God does not love everybody! God has mercy on whom he will have mercy, and whom he will he hardeneth. God told Pharaoh before he destroyed him, "For this same purpose have I raised thee up, that I might shew my power in thee, and that my name might be declared throughout all the earth." Rom. 9:17. Esteeming God's power, the vessels of mercy which he hath before prepared unto glory, know the riches of his grace in his kindness toward them through Jesus Christ. Many were told by Christ that they believed not, because they were not of God. Christ told his brethren that he that is of God heareth God's words. Brethren, God loves his children.

John 6:44. "No man can come to me, except the Father which hath sent me draw him: and I will raise him up at the last day." There are three powerful messages in this one verse of scripture. The natural man is not drawn to Christ. The flesh profits nothing, it is the Spirit that enlightens. We come to Christ only through the gift of the drawing power of God's Spirit. Those drawn to Christ will be raised up by him on the last day. Time will be no more after the last day, the day of resurrection when we hope to come forth anew in his image and after his likeness.

Lynwood Jacobs

2012

GEMS 7

Gems are verses of scripture that alone carry a powerful message to believers.

Matt. 23:15. "But woe unto you, scribes and Pharisees, hypocrites! for ye compass sea and land to make one proselyte, and when he is made, ye make him twofold more the child of hell than yourselves." Hypocrite: one who feigns to be other and better than he is, or a false pretender of piety. Hypocrisy: claiming to be what one is not. The Pharisees could not give up tradition. They insisted that even followers of Christ had to be circumcised and keep the Law of Moses in order to be saved. Modern Pharisees proselyte by insisting that they will save you if you accept Christ, stop sinning, and be baptized in the water of this world. Just as the hypocrites of old, they place a burden on others that neither they nor their forefathers were able to bear. If you are his, Christ made you acceptable to God when he bore your sins on the cross. When God puts his laws in your heart, and prints them in your mind, he becomes unto you the true and living God, and you become a manifest child to him. At the same time, Christ baptizes you with the Holy Ghost and with fire. It is a complete deal for the recipient of God's grace and mercy.

Romans 11:33. "O the depth of the riches both of the wisdom and knowledge of God! how unsearchable are his judgments, and his ways past finding out!" God's wisdom has made foolish the wisdom of this world. Solomon was filled with great wisdom of this world by God, but turned to the gods of his wives in his later years. (I Kings 3:12 & 11:4) Why? Because God destroys the wisdom of the wise, and brings to naught the understanding of the prudent. Somewhere along their journey here on earth, God gives to each one of his elect the Spirit of wisdom and revelation in the knowledge of him and Jesus Christ. To know them is to know eternal life, a gift of God through Christ. Isaiah said that the Lord is our judge. When Christ said judge righteous judgment, he is telling us to first look within, and examine ourselves.

Romans 11:5. "Even so then at this present time also there is a remnant according to the election of grace." At any point of time God has his "seven thousand" who have not bowed their knee to the image of Baal. They worship God in Spirit and in truth because they are the chosen, beloved children of God.

Romans 13:1. "Let every soul be subject unto the higher powers. For there is no power but of God: THE POWERS THAT BE ARE ORDAINED OF GOD!" This great truth is one that the natural man cannot accept. Those that have been made partakers of the power of the world to come understand that this is true because God is omnipotent! He is not the part-time, sometime begging, wishing, wanting, will-if-you-let him being that is presented to the world by those ordained to do so. I don't care what James implied to the twelve tribes of Israel, (James 5:20) NO MAN HAS EVER SAVED ANOTHER MAN'S SOUL! It is the power of God, Christ, and the Holy Ghost that was ordained of old to save the soul of every elect of God. Even the greatest events of the natural world are nothing more than fleeting moments in the ordained purpose of God. Two of those greatest events in modern history, WWI is almost forgotten, and WWII is fast fading in recall. The natural child was designed by God to live in the "now." His spiritual child was designed by God to live in the "forever."

I Cor. 12:3. "Wherefore I give you to understand, that no man speaking by the Spirit of God calleth Jesus accursed: and that no man can say that Jesus is the Lord, but by the Holy Ghost." How simple! The Holy Ghost is a gift of God. This Comforter blesses its possessor to say unto Christ," How great thou art, thou blessed son of God, our hope, our love, our friend and our precious saviour."

I Tim. 6:10. "For the love of money is the root of all evil: which while some have coveted after, they have erred from the faith, and pierced themselves through with many sorrows." This scripture explains why God's people are reluctant to pay money for a member's service to the Church. From the beginning of his Apostleship Paul urged those who could, to help the poor. (I Cor. 16:1-3) They did not have national income taxes and state sales taxes to support the poor and needy worldwide as we have today. From the beginning, the love of money raised its ugly head. Churches began to ask for money for this false cause and that false cause to the point that money, and not God's will, became the measure for many church functions. Churches not only paid their pastors, but out bid one another for an affiliated pastor's service. Monstrous temples, decorated with idols, became the preferred places of worship for those whose leaders claimed to have the power to do that which the Holy Ghost alone can accomplish. A simple service in a simple facility was frowned upon by many, yet there was more true worship of God and Christ in such places, as it is today.

Lynwood Jacobs

2012

GEMS 8

Gems are verses of scripture that alone carry a powerful message to believers.

I Peter 2:9. "But ye are a chosen generation, a royal priesthood, an holy nation, a peculiar people; that ye should shew forth the praises of him who hath called you out of darkness into his marvelous light." What a glorious hope that we are one of that chosen generation that existed in the mind and purpose of God before the foundation of the world. Surely, we have a desire to render praise, and honor, and glory to the great I AM. Members of a Royal Priesthood offer up spiritual sacrifices of praise toward God and Christ. The fruit of their lips render praise to them alone. A Holy nation is one whose ruler is King of Kings and Lord of Lords. The inhabitants of that Nation are a peculiar people who walk, not after the flesh, but after the Spirit. Their hope in Christ is foolishness to the world, but an anchor to their soul. They love one another and rejoice in Christ Jesus who is their eternal light. To them, this world is not their home, but they are as wayfaring pilgrims seeking a city with foundation whose builder and maker is God.

Psa. 133:1. "Behold, how good and how pleasant it is for the brethren to dwell together in unity!" For more than 50 years I have been blessed to go among those who worship that God whose will is absolute in all events in time and eternity. The Bible labels them *brethren* because they have the same parents as Jesus Christ. God is their Father, and Jerusalem which is above is their Mother. They love their elder Brother and those that God said, "I will be unto them a Father, and they shall be unto me sons and daughters." These know harmony in the Church because they love one

190

another, and find great joy in the presence of their brethren. To them the Church is not a court of law, but a place of sweet refuge from the law. Their unity is that of the Holy Spirit that unites them in love for one another.

Malachi 3:6. "For I am the Lord, I change not; therefore ye sons of Jacob are not consumed." Prayer, so called, that attempts to change God's mind is of no avail, regardless of how well intentioned. To me, that seems to be the purpose of some. Nothing can change the ordained will of an unchangeable God. When someone is facing trials or death, our hope for them should be that the Lord will reconcile them to his will. Then they can live or depart in peace.

Isaiah 2:1. "Behold my servant whom I uphold; mine elect, in whom my soul delighteth; I have put my Spirit upon him: he shall bring forth judgment to the Gentiles." God judges no man. He placed all judgment in the hands of Christ. There are those who receive power from Christ to bring forth righteous judgment on earth. Saul of Tarsus was ordained of God and changed by Christ to bring forth judgment as Paul, Apostle to the Gentiles. He was made to declare the judgment that we are all sinners by nature. The Spirit of the Lord was upon him to preach Christ crucified and risen from the dead, the only sin sacrifice acceptable to God. Paul was blessed to praise God, and declare the unsearchable riches of Christ to the Gentiles. Elect Gentiles are called by the Holy Spirit out of nature's darkness into the glorious liberty of those whose names are in the Book of Life.

Job 25:13. "By his spirit he hath garnished the heavens; his hand hath formed the crooked serpent." Yes, he has adorned the heavens with stars, planets, comets, black holes, love, and whatever else he desired. He formed the crooked serpent, the same serpent that appeared unto Adam and Eve in the Garden of Eden. God ordained that they would be tempted to make manifest what they were in the flesh, sinners. The truth does not tempt. It takes a lie to tempt. Since God, Christ, and the Holy Spirit are Truth, and cannot lie, God formed a lying spirit to tempt. God said eat and you will die, but the liar said eat and you won't die. They ate and were banished from the garden and their closeness to God. Today we call that serpent Satan, or the devil, or an evil spirit from the Lord, etc. He was a liar from the beginning and is still lying and tempting to fulfill the purpose of God according to election. (To say that Almighty God, the creator of heaven and earth, formed Adam and Eve, put them in Eden, and did not know what they would do, is ridiculous) Though God's chosen Saints are no better in the flesh than anyone else, his gift of love in their heart blesses them to live and walk in the way that leads unto life everlasting. Adam, a son of God, and Eve his wife had to be born again of the Spirit to become manifested children of the King, the same as their offspring.

Lynwood Jacobs

2012

GEMS 9

Gems are verses of scripture that alone have a powerful message for believers.

John 19:30. "When Jesus therefore had received the vinegar, he said, It is finished: and he bowed his head, and gave up the ghost." IT IS FINISHED. To me, these are three of the most important words ever spoken! Christ's terrible suffering on the cross is finished. His time on earth as Mary's son is finished. His work of redemption is established forever. His physical presence as Comforter, healer, friend, and loved one to his disciples has ended, to be replaced with his spiritual presence forever. After three days, he is to come forth in a spiritual body as King of Kings, and Lord of Lords, yea, as the risen Son of God, and beloved conqueror of death, hell, and the grave. God, what a wonderful Son you have there with you! He is alive, and his brethren love him. Thank you for such a sure savior.

John 17:23. "I in them, and thou in me, that they may be made perfect in one; and that the world may know that thou hast sent me, and hast loved them, as thou hast loved me." With Christ in you the hope of glory, and with God in Christ, means they have taken up their abode in you by the Holy Spirit. You are now possessed, and made perfect by the Three-in-One Godhead. You know that eternal love that was ever with the Father, but now is made manifest to his beloved children at his appointed time. God promised love in an eternal covenant with his Son, Christ paid for it on the cross, and the Holy Ghost alone delivers true love to God's beloved. O Lord, may we be counted in that number that dwells in love among your believing children.

I Cor. 13:1. "Though I speak with the tongues of men and of angels, and have not charity, I am become as sounding brass, or a tinkling symbol." Charity is a fruit of God's love, which is one of the fruits of God's Spirit. Without the gift of the Spirit all is vanity. The Apostle continued his dissertation on the importance of charity by saying, "And though I have the gift of prophecy, and understand all mysteries, and all knowledge; and though I have all faith, so that I could remove mountains, and have not charity, I am nothing." I knew of an old brother who claimed to be an expert on church discipline. He never mentioned that love for one another is the only discipline we need in the church, or out! No matter how smart we think we are, no matter how great we think our faith is, no matter how gifted we think we are, without charity we are nothing. To finish the Apostle's thoughts on our need for charity, "And though I bestow all my goods to feed the poor, and though I give my body to be burned, and have not charity, it profiteth me nothing." Peter bragged that he would lay down his life to protect Christ from his enemies. He had not yet received power from on high, or he would have known that Christ did not need him for protection. Throughout history, there have been believers and nonbelievers, poor and rich people, destructive and constructive weather, light and dark skin, food and famine, height and depth, great empires raised up and brought down by God, and many more of such oppositions. Thank God for all our known and unknown blessings.

Matt. 4:10. "Then saith Jesus unto him, Get thee hence, Satan: for it is written, Thou shalt worship the Lord thy God, and him only shalt thou serve." To some, this may be the most controversial scripture in the Bible. With his own hand God formed the crooked serpent (Job 26:13) that

194

Christ called Satan. Others have called him the devil, a lying spirit, an evil spirit, or Beelzebub. One of his most descriptive names is tempter (Matt.4:3), because tempting with lies is one way he serves the purpose of God, who cannot lie. God ordained that our fleshly mother Eve would be tempted of the crooked serpent in the very beginning, which led to the first recorded instance of transgression by man of a commandment of God. God had already ordained that Christ's redeeming blood, poured out on the cross, would pay for the sins of every child of God. Not one of them shall be forever lost, and I believe that includes our mother Eve. Though Satan and his children may believe there is one God, they cannot worship him in Spirit and in Truth. Only a Saint, a manifested child of God, can worship the one only living and true God and his beloved son, Jesus Christ.

Lynwood Jacobs

2012

GEMS 10

Gems are verses of scripture that alone have a powerful message for believers.

Eph. 1:11. "In whom also we have obtained an inheritance, being predestinated according to the purpose of him who worketh all things after the council of his own will:" To me, the book of Ephesians contains some of the greatest GEMS in the Bible. This verse tells us that our God is a God of eternal purpose, that all things come to pass after the council of his own will, and that according to his will his children are predestinated to be heirs and joint heirs with Christ of an inheritance that endureth forever. Such words are meant only for Saints of God.

I John 3:13. "Marvel not, my brethren, if the world hates you." The Apostles often reminded their brethren to manifest love for one another. Believers in Christ love their brethren. Non-believers have always hated them as they hated Christ when he was in the world. Saul of Tarsus hated Christ until he was born again to become the beloved Apostle Paul. Then persecution of the Jews almost destroyed Paul physically, but through all his pain and suffering for his belief in Christ, he was blessed to stand firm in his God given faith. There are many who claim to be Christians today, but fail the simplest tests. They deny the electing grace of God. Their pitiful savior begs, and wishes, and will-if-you let him. They can change their little god's mind if enough of them beg long enough and loud enough. They deny the manifested will of God in all events in time and eternity. Brethren, rejoice in your God-given belief in election, in your praise toward an unchangeable Godhead, and that God's will, not yours, is done in heaven and in earth. Don't be surprised if you are hated by some church goers.

Phil. 2:12. "Wherefore, my beloved, as ye have always obeyed, not as in my presence only, but now much more in my absence, work out your own salvation with fear and trembling." Some treat this as a command, but I believe it was a warning of failure from the Apostle Paul to his beloved brethren. If they were able to work out their own salvation successfully, it would have brought joy and rejoicing, not fear and trembling. In the next verse the Apostle Paul tells us that it is not you, but God who does the work, "For it is God which worketh in you both to will and to do of his good pleasure." The result of God's work brings joyful hope and eternal salvation to his child. Anyone who claims personal credit for their eternal salvation blasphemes the Holy Ghost by denying the power thereof. Eternal life is a gift of God.

Matt. 8:25. "And his disciples came to him, and awoke him, saying, Lord save us: we perish." This is an example of salvation in time, ordained by God. First, they appealed to Christ. Second, they begged him to save their natural lives. Third, though they may have had little faith, they knew enough to ask help of the only one on the ship that could help them. It was God's will that they be saved so Christ rebuked the winds and sea and there was a great calm. Another example occurred when Christ bade Peter to come to him by walking on the water. Peter was doing fine until he became afraid, and he began to sink. Peter cried out, Lord save me. Peter appealed to Christ. He begged Christ to save his natural life, the only one that could help him. It was God's will that Peter not die, so Jesus caught Peter by the hand and saved him. Abraham Lincoln said, "I have been driven to my knees many times because there

197

was no place else to go." Haven't we all cried out to God or Christ when there was no place else to go.

2 Cor. 6:16. "And what agreement hath the temple of God with idols? For ye are the temple of the living God; as I have said, I will dwell in them, and walk in them; and I will be their God, and they shall be my people." Yes, you may be the one physically walking, but it will be God in you who is directing your steps in paths of righteousness for his names sake. Why? Because your body has become a temple of the Holy Ghost, which you have of God, and you are not your own, for ye are bought with a price, therefore glorify God in your body and Spirit which are God's. The glory that God gave unto Christ, Christ has given unto you, if you are numbered in those, "And I will be a Father unto you, and ye shall be my sons and daughters, saith the Lord Almighty." (2 Cor. 6:18) Your preparation as a Saint of God is readying you to go HOME.

Lynwood Jacobs

July 2012

THE WAY

There is a way that seemeth right unto a man, but the end thereof are the ways of death. (Prov. 16:25) When man's heart deviseth his way it is the way of death. When God directs man's steps by His Spirit it is the way of life. (See Prov. 16:4) Then man's steps may be on that highway, and in that way called the way of Holiness. (See Isa. 35:8) God's children believe that Christ is the way of Holiness, because no man comes to the Father, but by Him. (See John 14:16) Man's way is the self-righteous way that leads unto death because it blasphemes the Holy Ghost by denying the power thereof. Only the power of the Holy Spirit can reveal that pathway that leads unto life everlasting. (See I Cor. 2:12.) This revelation is given only to those that have been born again of God. (See John 1:13.)

There is a glorious city, the City of God, awaiting at the end of the way that leads to that eternal Home for the beloved of the Lord. (See Psalm 87:3.) Christ knows that way because He has gone on before, and is now in that beautiful city awaiting the Father's date to go bring God's children home. (See Mark 16:19.) Then the ransomed of the Lord shall return, and come to that glorious city with songs and everlasting joy upon their heads: they shall obtain joy and gladness, and sorrow and sighing shall flee away. (See Isa. 35:10) Think of it! No more tears, no more sorrow and sadness, no more separation, no more need for faith and hope. The ransomed of the Lord return because they were chosen IN Him before the world began. They were IN Him when He came out from God and came into the world, they were IN Him when He hung on the cross, they were IN Him when He arose from the dead and left the world to go unto the Father.

What a great joy it is to trust that we, too, though unworthy, are still IN Him as we are on our way home to that wonderful Family of God reunion in the sky. With astonished eyes the Saints will then see as they are seen and know as they are known. If we are counted in that number, we will not only see our precious Saviour Jesus Christ, the Son of God, but we will behold the Holiest of the Holy, the GOD of this universe, our everlasting FATHER sitting upon the throne of His glory. (See I Cor. 15: 24-28.) In company with our beloved elder Brother, who has made the way, and with the Angels of God and Saints out of every nation and time, we will honor and glorify God through an everlasting, glorious rapture in a world that shall never end.

Lynwood Jacobs

April 2008

JUDGMENT

Recently, I read John 5:22 where Christ said, "For the Father judgeth no man, but hath committed all judgment unto the Son." I said wait a minute. Didn't Isaiah say in the 33rd chapter that God is our judge, God is our lawgiver, God is our king, He will save us? Of course, that is not what Isaiah said. "For the Lord is our judge, the Lord is our lawgiver, the Lord is our king, He will save us." Isaiah was telling us that Christ would be our judge, our lawgiver, our king and savior.

God ordained that Moses would bring the old laws written on tables of stone. God ordained that His Son would write the new law on fleshy tables of the heart, and imprint it in the mind of His brethren. It is called the Law of the Spirit of Life in Christ Jesus. This law of LOVE rules, by measure of God's will, the actions of a child born of God. Without God's love in our heart, all else is vanity and vexation of spirit.

God ordained that Christ would come out from the Father and come into the world to save His people from their sins. Isaiah was blessed to declare this hundreds of years before Christ's advent on earth to give eternal life to as many as the Father had given Him. These are the same ones that God chose in His Son before the world began.

To Isaiah, Christ was his Lord of Lords and King of Kings, just as He is to those today who worship Him in spirit and in truth. Christ took up His spiritual abode in Isaiah, in exactly the same way as He must take up His abode in us. Isaiah could know that Jesus Christ would come only through the revealing power of the Holy Ghost.

Christ judges righteous judgment because He does the Father's will, and not His own. We judge righteous judgment when we are blessed of Christ to love as He loved, and to manifest the fruits of love in our daily thoughts and actions. There are those who judge me harshly because they say that what I preach "makes God the author of sin." In the first place it is the silliest statement that the devil ever came up with. In the second place some of the ablest writers on the omnipotent power of God have been thrown into some kind of tizzy when accused of "making God the author of sin." They then start to "defend God" and usually wind up denying His sovereignty that they have so ably declared. They may even call God a liar. My hope is that when speaking of God my brethren will use the word creator, and forget the word author. Create means to bring into existence. My God is the only creator, the only cause, all the rest are results. If He is not your God, so be it. For me, I believe that God is my creator, that Christ is my judge, and I hope my lawgiver, King and Savior.

Lynwood Jacobs

June 2009, Revised

A LITTLE LEAVEN LEAVENS THE WHOLE LUMP

Gal. 5:9

Published in <u>Zion's Landmark</u>

August, 1975

I believe that God purposed that the Apostle Paul sound this great warning, not only to the Galatian churches, but to the Church in this day too. "All scripture is given by inspiration of God and is profitable for doctrine, for reproof, for correction, for instruction in righteousness: That the man of God may be perfect, thoroughly furnished unto all good works." (II Tim. 3:16, 17) Whether or not God purposed that we in this day heed this warning remains to be seen. His will directs our thoughts and actions. "...I have purposed it, I will also do it." (Isa. 46:11) For this scripture to bear fruit in our lives, God must have purposed that we obey from the heart His warning to the Church—a little leaven leavens the whole lump.

Christ warned His disciples to take heed and beware of that leaven that had nothing to do with bread. "Take heed and beware of the leaven of the Pharisees and of the Sadducees. How is it that ye do not understand that I spake it not to you concerning bread, that ye should beware of the leaven of the Pharisees and of the Sadducees. Then understood they how that He bade them not beware of the leaven of bread, but of the Pharisees and Sadducees." (Matt. 16:6, 11, 12)

My hope is that God will bless me to write about some of the leaven that can or has crept into our own doctrine and practice. (I am not concerned here with the Campbellites, conditionalists, free-willers, etc. who could not heed the Truth, even if I were blessed to declare it) If we have been ordained to see and to omit or cast out this leaven, then we will not come under the condemnation, "foolish Galatians, who hath bewitched you, that ye should not obey the truth…" (Gal. 3:1)

I believe the Apostle Paul used the term leaven to describe false beliefs that lead to false teachings or doctrine and to empty practices in the church. In this context, the scope of this one scripture becomes overwhelming. It reaches from Genesis to Revelation in the Bible and covers our daily lives whether in the church or out. For this reason, I hope this writing will be bathed in the light of the Apostle Peter's admonition, "If any man speak, let him speak as the oracles of God…" (I Peter 4:11) The enlightened scriptures must be our guide, Christ must be our way, and experience must reinforce our learning, if we are to contrast the unleavened bread of the Truth with the old leaven of the law and of malice and wickedness. (See I Cor. 5:8.)

The Apostle warns that a little leaven leavens the whole lump. If we look about us we can see the astonishing results of this truth. Watch a church that has had a little leaven creep into the doctrine of predestination. Absolute predestination becomes limited predestination as God's sovereignty becomes limited sovereignty. Then predestination in any form becomes a forbidden subject. Man's works soon become mixed with God's Grace. The congregation is exhorted to exercise the Spirit, rather than hop and pray that the Spirit of God will exercise the congregation. The doctrine of God's electing grace soon fails to stir their hearts though the words may be mouthed occasionally. Good works become the fruits of the innate ability of man and not the fruits of the Holy Spirit of God. "Water salvation," in the waters of this world soon replaces eternal salvation found only in the River of Life.

In time, the last old mother and father in Israel pass on. Any restraints they may have been given to exercise are gone. Then the whole barrel rots before your eyes. Rather than die a merciful death, the church begins to "revive" as warm bodies, and not warm hearts, are added to the membership. Money demands increase. Vanity rules the day as the flesh is satisfied in doctrine and practice, and the shepherds feed themselves. (See Jer. 34:1-6.)

Christ's words perfectly describe this new church, "…for ye are like unto whited sepulchers, which indeed appear beautiful outward, but are within full of dead men's bones and of all uncleanness. Even so ye also outwardly appear righteous unto men, but within ye are full of hypocrisy and iniquity." (Matt. 23:27:28)

From the above picture, it should be easily understood why even this lowly sinner hopes that God will bless him and those he has been given a love for to heed this great warning. A little leaven can and does leaven the whole lump. The severity of the results from not heeding this clarion call to solidarity in love, doctrine, and practice, removes any fear that I may step on someone's toes. I have found that the Truth not only pinches my toes, it crushes my very being. It explodes my notions and ideas, and they become myths in a vapor that soon pass away. But the Truth shall stand forever. It is the same yesterday, today, and forever.

Love the Foundation—
Doctrine the Food

God's everlasting love is the foundation upon which He has built His church, not doctrine. It is His love that draws the saints to God, to Christ, and to one another. "Yea, I have loved thee with an everlasting love: therefore, with loving kindness have I drawn thee." (Jer. 31:3) "We love Him, because He first loved us." (I John 4:19) "Beloved, let us love one another: for love is of God; and everyone that loveth is born of God and knoweth God." (I John 4:7)

Doctrine feeds the child of God that has been born of God and drawn to the church by love. The only food that nourishes one is the Truth. "I am the bread of life; he that cometh to Me shall never hunger." (John 6:35) Love is the one ingredient that can never be missing if we are to obey from the heart that form of doctrine which Christ delivered to the church. (See Rom. 6:17) "If you love me, keep My commandments. If a man love me, he will keep My words." (John 14:15, 23)

The beginning of God's love in a sinner's heart is the new birth. This must come before precept upon precept of His ways can be heard with a hearing ear, seen with a seeing eye, or understood with an understanding heart. Otherwise, words of truth fall on deaf ears, blind eyes, and a stony heart, there to wither and die without root. We must be rooted and grounded in love to comprehend with all saints and to know the love of Christ, which passeth knowledge, that we might be filled with all the fullness of God. (See Eph. 3:18, 19.)

My belief that love for the brethren, for Christ, and for God precedes true love for doctrine is based not only on the scriptures, but on experience. I once went into the water and baptized a brother who knew nothing about Primitive Baptist doctrine and belief. One day he came to visit a church that I served, seemingly because of a promise that he had made to himself two years before. This little church was basking in God's love and peace after a period of great trial. When a song was sung at the regular time for the reception of members, this brother came forward. We were surprised, of course, but not nearly so much as the brother himself. When asked to speak to the church, he couldn't. What was he to say, "I don't know why I am here?" When I asked him if he wanted a home in the church and to be a candidate for baptism, he could only shake his head to say, "Yes." By faith, the church was blessed to grant his wish.

Today, this brother serves that church and two others and is one of the ablest gifts we have ever had. Over the years, God has taught him the doctrine we rejoice to hear, and he has been blessed of God to preach the truth in love. Yet, he would be the first to testify that it was Grace, Love, and Mercy that brought him home, not doctrine.

At one time, I believe I liked doctrine more than I did the brethren and worshipped doctrine more than I did God. It was a head knowledge of words and not the heart knowledge of Christ that I desire today. I have argued the doctrine of predestination with the devil himself, not realizing at the time that it was a case of Satan bearing witness to Satan.

Experience has taught me that doctrine alone is not enough. Love must be the bond that unites us. It is the Rock upon which our doctrine and practice stand unswerving. Love for the brethren, for Christ, for God, as well as for sound doctrine is the completeness of God in Christ that I need. Hopefully, God has removed from my heart the leaven in that most beautiful and precious commandment that has become all my salvation and all my desire—to love and be loved as Christ loved.

Love draws people to the church. Doctrine feeds them after they have come home.

An Elder Is a Servant and Brother and Nothing More

In the mind of some, calling a pastor is like a marriage between him and the church. This is a concept that I believe is in error and that can cause serious trouble. Every true church is married to Christ, the King of Kings and Lord of Lords. "Wherefore, my brethren, ye also are become dead to the law by the body of Christ; that ye should be married to another, even to Him who is raised from the dead, that we should bring forth fruit unto God." (Rom. 7:4) Why should any church commit adultery by marrying her servant? According to Elder Calvin Harward, the late Elder Sam Atkinson of High Point, N. C., expressed my belief in what might be called the hierarchy of the church—the elders are at the bottom, the deacons next, the church is over both elders and deacons, and Christ is over all of it.

Look at the results of turning this order around. If the elder is at the top, Christ is at the bottom. This is not in keeping with my beliefs or understanding. Yet, I have seen, not only churches, but whole associations that have drifted dangerously close to this latter order. "That's Elder _____'s church or association." Any church or association that follows some man as their head is not going to die. I believe it is already dead. The church belongs to Christ. He is the head and no other. "And hath put all things under His feet and gave Him to be the head over ALL things to the church, which is His body, the fullness of Him that filleth all in all." (Eph. 1:22, 23) "And when He putteth forth His own sheep, He goeth before them, and the sheep follow Him, for they know His voice. And a stranger will they not follow, BUT WILL FLEE FROM HIM: For they know not the voice of strangers." (John 10:4, 5)

I believe each church owes their elder a two-fold measure of love—as a brother and as a servant—nothing more. I have never known a true church that could not pay this debt. This double measure of love is my great need and desire in the church. May Almighty God keep me from mistaking it for anything but what it is—love and not obedience.

By experience I have learned to trust in the collective judgment of a church over my own judgment. God has given me a deep trust in the Spiritual judgment He reveals unto those I hope are

208

my brethren. Any elder or member who thinks he is smarter than the church is exalted and shall be abased. I speak from experience. This belief does not stop me from expressing my feelings about matters, but it does make me respect the wishes of the church over my own wishes when they differ.

I believe that God ordained elders to serve His church. They are servants to the church, not God. He does not need to hear the truth declared. He is the Truth. God does not need to have the ordinances of the church administered to Himself. The church serves God, and elders serve the church. If elders are servants to God alone, they are beholden to Him only. But I believe that they are servants to the church, raised up by God's will for this purpose, and they are beholden to the church. I believe this concept is of great importance to peace in Zion.

Ecclesiastical Authority On Earth

I have heard it said that the individual churches are the highest ecclesiastical authority on earth. The truth is that individual churches are the ONLY ecclesiastical authority on earth, established as such by the highest ecclesiastical authority in heaven, Almighty God. "And if he shall neglect to hear them, tell it unto the church: but if he neglects to hear the church, let him be unto thee as an heathen and a publican." (Matt. 18:17)

The question arises then, how many does it take to constitute this ecclesiastical authority? The answer is two or more. "Again I say unto you, that if two of you shall agree on earth as touching anything that they shall ask, it shall be done for them of My Father which is in heaven." (Matt. 18:17, 19)

Once a problem has been presented to a church of two or more members, the collective judgment of that church is the only pertinent ecclesiastical authority to deal with that problem. This authority cannot be delegated to another body. If it is usurped by some other group, it is done so contrary to the Holy order established by Almighty God. "Let all things be done decently and in order." (I Cor. 14:40) I believe this means to let all things be done in love following God's order and not in strife following man's notions. When wrath enters the door of a church and it is met head on by greater wrath, nothing but vain jangling can follow. When wrath walks in the door and it is met head on by the collective love of a true church, there is nothing for wrath to do but flee. "And above all things have fervent charity among yourselves: for charity shall cover the multitude of sins." (I Peter 4:8) "For the wrath of man worketh not the righteousness of God." (Jam. 1:20) "Submit yourselves therefore to God. Resist the devil, and he will flee from you." (James 4:7) The only power that can resist Satan is the love of God shed abroad in a heart by the Holy Ghost, which is given of God. (See Rom. 5:5.)

Go to an association in which the ecclesiastical authority of the individual churches is being usurped by the association. There is no peace and little joy in such a meeting for me. Then go to an association where no ecclesiastical authority is exercised. Joy abounds for me, love is without dissimulation to me, and a peace prevails that passes all understanding. Does this not tell me something? Or am I so correct in all my thoughts and ways that I dare reject the words of the precious One who bought me with His blood, if I am His. A little leaven leavens the whole lump. May God bless us to recognize and follow His ways.

This brings up the question, how do we deal with problems between sister churches? Follow Matt. 18:15-20, but do so outside the annual associational meeting. These were set up by our forefathers as an ingathering of churches to rejoice together in song, prayer, preaching, and fellowship one with the other. One of the most despicable things to me is for my association to issue a general invitation to brethren of like faith and order to meet with us and then present them with the spectacle of the association exercising ecclesiastical authority that it does not have or carrying on some dogfight that should be omitted altogether, if possible, or at least held at some other time and place, if it must occur.

If a problem arises between two churches, let them meet as outlined in Matt. 18:15. If their problem cannot be reconciled, let them follow Matt. 18:16 by bringing in a sister church or two. If reconciliation still is not made, let all the churches directly involved meet to consider the matter with the entire membership being present or by delegates. (See Matt. 18:17.) BUT LET THESE MEETINGS BE SPECIAL and not be a part of the annual association.

My prayer to God is that when brethren from near and far visit the annual South Louisiana, Primitive and Union Associations of Texas, that they will find love, good food, wonderful singing, able preaching, great joy and delight in one another, AND NOTHING MORE. I have lost any desire that I might ever have had to promote the devil's work at our associations.

Lynwood Jacobs

(To Be Continued)

September, 1975

Absolute Predestination—The Foundation of God's Doctrine

Just as love is the foundation upon which God built His church, I believe absolute predestination is the foundation upon which He built His doctrine. Remove the foundation of the omnipotent power and absolute will of God in all events in time and eternity and the rest of the doctrine will crumble into a confused rubble. All things then become a mish-mash of happenstance, rather than an orderly occurrence of events ordered in all things and sure by the perfect will of a perfect Workman. "... He is the rock, His work is perfect." Without absolute predestination, eternal life is an empty hope, election becomes man's choice, grace is a sometimes thing, and the principles of the doctrine of Christ are nothing more than fuel for debates.

God is omnipotent, which means He is unlimited in power and authority. "...for the Lord God omnipotent reignth." (Rev. 19:8) His reign is unlimited in heaven and earth and is not subject to the will, desire, or understanding of any creature in heaven or in earth. "...and He doeth His will in the army of heaven and among the inhabitants of the earth and none can stay His hand or say unto Him, what doest thou?" (Dan. 4:35)

God is absolute. He is free from limit, restriction, and qualification. He either predestinated all things or nothing. His sovereignty is absolute or non-existent. Being absolute, He could not will some events in time and eternity and not will all events. (Some say He chooses to wait around to find out what is going to happen next. How foolish)

To me, the greatest leaven ever placed in the doctrine of absolute predestination is found in the London Confession of Faith. This Confession of Faith is one of the most remarkable collections of truth and error that has ever been compiled in the name of religion. Though fact outweighs fiction, and profound understanding tends to hide the myths and notions therein, yet its true beauty shines out of darkness, and its clarity is marred by confusion. God alone knows why such a potentially great work contains so much leaven. It has some of the most beautiful and profound statements outside the Bible so that many of the writers must have been inspired by the Holy Spirit. It also contains some equally profound contradictions so that Satan must have been at the writer's table also. Many of our churches and associations took their articles of faith directly or indirectly from the London Confession of Faith. I believe that in a few cases some tares were pulled with the wheat.

The Confession states that God decreed all things, then states that He did not decree anything.

Truth: "God hath decreed in Himself from all eternity, by the most wise and holy counsel of His own will, freely and unchangeable, all things whatsoever come to pass;" (Art. 1, Chapter 3) {in part}.

Error: "Although God knoweth whatsoever may or can come to pass upon all supposed conditions, yet hath He not decreed anything, because He foresaw it as future, or as that which would come to pass upon such conditions." (Art. 2, Chapter 3.[It is one eternal now with God.])

In the above two statements, I believe the writers of the truth worshiped an absolute God, and the writers of the error worshiped a limited god. Hopefully, I worship the one only living and true God who is absolute. No limited god can reach my case, so I have no desire to worship such, or be identified with those who do. Their god is not my God. Even so, I hope and deeply desire that this is spoken in love from a broken and contrite heart.

The writers listed many of the divine attributes of God stating emphatically that He is most absolute and works all things according to His own immutable will and council. Then they attempted to limit and restrict His immutable council and will.

Truth: "The Lord our God is…most absolute, working all things according to the council of His own immutable and most righteous will…" (Art. 1, Chapter 2 [in part])

Error: "…yet, so as thereby is God neither the author of sin, nor hath fellowship with any therein; nor is violence offered to the will of the creature, nor yet is the liberty of contingency of second causes taken away, but rather established, in which appears His wisdom in disposing all things, and power and faithfulness in accomplishing His decree." (Art. 1, Chapter 3, in part)

Of all the leaven in the London Confession of Faith, probably none exceeds that contained in this last statement. Men have gone to great lengths to defend the statement. "…yet so as thereby is God neither the author of sin." I once heard a man say that he had worried about the statement until he was given this thought: "God is not the author of sin, because He is under no law, so He cannot sin." Such a thought is so superfluous as to be little short of being foolish. Who in the church has ever accused God of sinning? I can't find where even Satan has accused God of sinning. They accused His Son, yes, but not God the Father. Why then is a statement required that says God is not a sinner, if indeed that is what the words mean.

The word **author** means creator which is the only way the word can be reasonably applied to God the Creator. "For by Him were ALL things created, that are in heaven, and that are in earth, visible and invisible, whether they be thrones, or principalities, or powers; ALL things were created by Him, and for Him:" (Col. 1:16)

To create means to bring into existence or being. For sin to come into existence, a weak, vain, and lustful human being subject to a law and a liar had to be created.

I am a sinner and need to be forgiven for my sins, one who is ten thousand talents in debt without a farthing to pay. My need to be forgiven for my sins is not the end of my need for Christ. Rather it is the beginning of my total need for Him.

Sin is the outward manifestation of my inward weakness. I not only need forgiveness for sins, I need inward strength. My need for Christ is not based on sin alone, if I am a child of God. He has forgiven the sins of His people. "For I will be merciful to their unrighteousness, and their sins and their iniquities will I remember no more." (Heb. 8:12) My need for Christ is because of my stony heart.

Sin is the stench that flows from my corrupted being. I not only need forgiveness for sin, I need incorruption. My need for Christ is because of my corruptible being.

Sin measures my inability to resist Satan's temptations. I need to be delivered from the power of Satan into the glorious liberty of the children of God.

Sin shows the midnight darkness of my blind soul. I need light to shine out of that darkness and eyes to see that light in others.

I need Christ to change my soul, spirit, and body; to put off the old man and put on the new. I need strength, incorruption and wisdom from above. I need Him to shod my feet with preparation of the gospel of peace, to gird my loins about with truth, to be my breastplate of righteousness, and my helmet of salvation. I need Him to be my way, my stay and staff, my husband, friend, and brother.

Above all I need Christ to be the Lord my Righteousness, my all in all, that I might love and be loved as He loved. "Forgive me, Oh Lord! Then deliver me from the body of this death. Save me or I perish!" is my cry.

I have at this moment no desire to deny my very being nor ask of Him, "Why hast thou made me thus?" My hope is that He has given me a desire to understand a revealed measure of His works, not question them nor try to limit Him in anything. God is not now, nor has He ever been, nor will He ever be a begging, pleading, restricted, limited, or conditional God. All events in time and eternity are the orderly disposal of the will and desire of a perfect Creator. May He bless me to rest my case on this foundation.

There is but one cause—Almighty God. The rest are results.

Because God formed man weak in the flesh, the result is that man is weak in the flesh. Because God gives His people inward strength through Jesus Christ, the result is their strength through Him.

Because God made man subject to vanity, the result is that the natural man has a soul that is empty and without Spiritual fruit. Because God frees His people from vanity by the gift of the Holy Spirit, the result is that they that have the Spirit do manifest the fruits of the Spirit.

Because God formed man mortal and corruptible, the result is that man is mortal and corruptible. Because God gave His people the victory through Jesus Christ, the result is that they shall put on immortality and incorruption.

Because God gave man a holy law that none could keep to a jot and tittle, the result is that all are lawbreakers. Because Christ kept and fulfilled the law to a jot and tittle, the result is that His brethren are not under the law, but under grace.

Because God formed Satan to lie and to tempt, the result is that Satan lies and tempts. Because God gave Christ the power to destroy Satan and His works, the result is that Christ destroyed the power of Satan over His people. I believed Satan's lies, not because I thought they were the truth, but because I knew nothing else. With the Apostle Paul, I did it ignorantly, and in unbelief. Now, if I am what I hope I am, that excuse has ended. If He keeps me by faith, no longer do I yield to every temptation. If His strength is mine, by measure of the gift of Christ, it is sufficient.

Because God made man subject to a carnal mind, the result is that all are carnal, sold under sin. Because God gives His people a Spiritual mind, the result is that they have life and peace and freedom from sin in Jesus Christ.

Because God created every human being to sin, the result is that all have sinned and come short of the glory of God. If God was not the creator of sin, who was? It shows me my total need for Jesus Christ, for which hopefully I am thankful.

I don't know what the writers of the London Confession of Faith meant when they stated that God has no fellowship for sinners. The truth is that those who are dead in sin have no fellowship with God. When quickened by Him, even when dead in sin, by faith, hope and charity we find peace with God and the end everlasting life.

"God's wisdom in disposing all things, and power and faithfulness in accomplishing His decrees," does not appear in second causes, but appears in the MANIFESTED decrees, promises, and gifts of a covenant keeping triune Godhead. There is no such thing as second causes or other causes, which are nothing more than the results of God's Holy purpose which He purposed in His righteous will and Self before the world was.

■ ■

The spirit exercises the child of God. The child of God does not exercise the Spirit.

"The doctrine of this high mystery of predestination is to be handled with special prudence and care; that men, attending the will of God revealed in His word, and yielding obedience thereunto, may from the certainty of their effectual vocation be assured of their eternal election: so shall this doctrine afford matter of praise, reverence and admiration of God, and of humility, diligence and abundant consolation to all that sincerely obey the gospel." (Art. 7, Chapter 3)

This whole article is so foreign to my understanding, and contrary to my belief that I fear to even try to comment on it.

Hopefully God will give me the great measure of charity I need to do so.

My only comment on the word **handled** is that the power of God "handles" the doctrine, not man.-

Mankind does not attend the will of God, but does the will of God. His people do the will of God revealed in their heart and experience, and attested to by the Bible, not vice versa.

There is no certainty in anything in this life with reference to my effectual vocation. The only certainty is that what God doeth, it shall be forever. Nothing can be put to it, nor anything taken from it.

I have no assurance of eternal election, but I hope to have a hope in an eternally electing God. I cannot volunteer humility. If so, it would be a voluntary humility that every child of God could see through and know it for what it was—the fruits of the flesh. If I am humble, it is because God has abased me. I have exalted myself as high as the eagle and made my nest among the stars, but He has abased me, I hope.

Doctrine does not afford praise, admiration, and reverence of God. They that worship God in Spirit and in Truth praise, honor and glorify Him.

God's people do not obey the gospel; they obey love in Christ. The new commandment is with power. It does not beg for obedience, but the will of God demands obedience and the power of God grants both the faith and the obedience of faith to His people.

The Lord Jesus Christ Himself and God even the Father has given everlasting consolation and good hope through grace unto His people. This is a living hope in a living God given to a living people who are alive unto God through Jesus Christ. May I be counted in the number!

The doctrine of absolute predestination was given by God to His Church for understanding. The unregenerated who use it only as a stump to hide their foolishness do so to the just condemnation to which they were ordained.

"Teach me, O Lord, the way of Thy statutes; and I shall keep it to the end. Give me understanding, and I shall keep Thy law: yea, I shall observe it with my whole heart. Make me to go in the path of Thy commandments; for therein do I delight. Incline my heart unto Thy testimonies, and not to covetousness. Turn away mine eyes from beholding vanity; and quicken thou me in the way." (Psalms 119:33-37)

Lynwood Jacobs

LAW

A law is a rule of action. When the law of the Spirit of Life in Christ Jesus rules our actions, the result is good works. When the law of sin and death rules our actions, the result is dead works. When God's love in our heart and mind rules our actions we love God, Christ, and one another. When "love God and thy neighbor" is written only on tablets of stone, and not in our heart, we can't even keep the first two mandates of the law that was given by Moses. When the law of faith, which worketh by love, rules our actions it gives true substance to the things hoped for, such as the life and immortality promised through Jesus Christ. When the law of unbelief rules our actions, we may deny the very existence of God and Christ.

The word law in the Bible may have more than one motivator. The motivator of our action may be personal, such as love or hate, or it may be general, such as peace or war. The overseers of the law that was given by Moses are the Levitical priesthood, whose high priest was from the tribe of Levi. The overseer of the law of grace and truth that came by Christ, is the Holy Ghost, and Jesus Christ himself is the High Priest.

Christ was the end of the law for righteousness to everyone that would be given to believe in Him. From the beginning of time, there was never a law given that could give eternal life. Christ said of His brethren, I give unto them eternal life and they shall never perish. What He said was true in the beginning, and it is true today.

True doctrine that rules our thoughts and actions exalts God and Christ, and abases man. False doctrine that rules our thoughts and actions exalts man, and abases God and

Christ. The devil's doctrine attempts to exalt God and man equally, which results in a half sheep, half goat, part works, part grace, part man, part God theology that would confuse the very elect, if that were possible.

If you are blessed, love God, love Christ, and love one another. All the rest will take care of itself according to the manifested will of God.

Lynwood Jacobs

May 2011

ADAM

Dear Brother J.M.,

I enjoyed your writing about whether Adam was a born again child of God. As you tell me sometimes, "You just didn't finish it."

Adam was a son of God. (Luke 3:38) The Apostle Paul said that as many as are led by the Spirit of God, they are the sons of God. (See Rom. 8:14.) Since Adam was a son of God, he was led by the Spirit of God. Adam had to have the Spirit in order to be led of the Spirit. In order to have the Spirit he had to be born again of God like any child of the King.

Adam was a child of God because he was a son of God. The Apostle Paul said that we are children of God by faith in Christ Jesus. (See Gal. 3:26.) Adam believed in Christ according to the workings of God's mighty power, just as any child of God. Also, as a child of God, Adam was delivered from the bondage of corruption into the glorious liberty of the children of God. (See Rom. 8:21.)

With such evidence why would anyone doubt Adam's birthright?

Lynwood Jacobs

March 2009